NEW DIRECTIONS FOR ADULT AND CONTINUING EDUCATION

Susan Imel, *Ohio State University*
Ralph G. Brockett, *University of Tennessee, Knoxville*
EDITORS-IN-CHIEF

New Perspectives on Designing and Implementing Effective Workshops

Jean Anderson Fleming
Ball State University

EDITOR

Number 76, Winter 1997

JOSSEY-BASS PUBLISHERS
San Francisco

NEW PERSPECTIVES ON DESIGNING AND IMPLEMENTING EFFECTIVE WORKSHOPS
Jean Anderson Fleming (ed.)
New Directions for Adult and Continuing Education, no. 76
Susan Imel, Ralph G. Brockett, Editors-in-Chief

Microfilm copies of issues and articles are available in 16mm and 35mm, as well as microfiche in 105mm, through University Microfilms Inc., 300 North Zeeb Road, Ann Arbor, Michigan 48106-1346.

ISSN 1052-2891   ISBN 0-7879-1163-1

NEW DIRECTIONS FOR ADULT AND CONTINUING EDUCATION is part of The Jossey-Bass Higher and Adult Education Series and is published quarterly by Jossey-Bass Inc., Publishers, 350 Sansome Street, San Francisco, California 94104-1342. Periodicals postage paid at San Francisco, California, and at additional mailing offices. Postmaster: Send address changes to New Directions for Adult and Continuing Education, Jossey-Bass Inc., Publishers, 350 Sansome Street, San Francisco, California 94104-1342.

SUBSCRIPTIONS cost $54.00 for individuals and $90.00 for institutions, agencies, and libraries.

EDITORIAL CORRESPONDENCE should be sent to the Editor-in-Chief, Susan Imel, ERIC/ACVE, 1900 Kenny Road, Columbus, Ohio 43210–1090. E-mail: imel.1@osu.edu.

Cover photograph by Wernher Krutein/PHOTOVAULT © 1990.

Jossey-Bass Web address: http://www.josseybass.com

Printed in the United States of America on acid-free recycled paper containing 100 percent recovered waste paper, of which at least 20 percent is postconsumer waste.

CONTENTS

Editors' Notes

The workshop is the workhorse of adult and continuing education. According to the *American Heritage Dictionary* (1992, p. 2057), a workhorse is "something . . . that performs dependably under heavy or prolonged use. . . ." Although we will never be certain when the first workshop was conducted, we can be certain that workshops have been used for the education of adults for decades and perhaps much longer. As editor of the first sourcebook on this topic in 1984, Thomas J. Sork notes that we are often tempted to describe workshops as *"omnipresent and ubiquitous"* (p. 3, emphasis in the original). Although he continues to explain that this perception may be due to the imprecision with which the term is used, nevertheless workshops are routine events in our practice of adult and continuing education. They have been heavily used for a long time and are relied on for meeting a variety of adult learning needs quickly and effectively. We depend on this workhorse of our practice. The authors of this sourcebook examine how we treat this workhorse, from conception to completion, to ensure that we can continue to depend on it to meet the learning needs and expectations of adults now and into the future.

Our dependence on workshops calls for precision in how we use the term. We are committed to "doing workshops" well, which means we must first understand what they are, what purposes and needs they meet, and what we and learners can expect from them. Sork (1984) agrees that "conceptual clarity can help improve discussions of workshops" (p. 3). He contrasts definitions of workshops offered in the 1960s with those offered twenty years later in the 1980s, noting a declining clarity and precision in the more recent definitions. The description offered here is similar to Sork's own definition and to the myriad others that have preceded and succeeded it. The focus here is on distinguishing and highlighting those characteristics that make a workshop what it should be, that is, those features that a workshop must have to be considered effective. In one form or another, all the authors in this volume have noted these distinguishing characteristics. Discussions with colleagues, my own experiences, and a review of several sources (Bergevin, Morris, and Smith, 1963; Bourner, Martin, and Race, 1955; Caffarella, 1994; Knowles, 1980; Nowlen, 1980; Sork, 1984; Szcypkowski, 1980) led to the description offered here.

The purpose of a workshop is to develop the individual competence of participants within a specific, well-defined area of need; emphasis is usually placed on the transfer and application of new learning. More specifically, a workshop provides for hands-on practice, thus giving it the character of a laboratory. A workshop is designed to be highly interactive and to support participants learning from one another; it is never an "information dump." A resource person in the role of workshop leader, however, provides information that may be required. Often a workshop results in a product that participants take with them, and the word *practical* frequently comes into the conversation when workshops are mentioned. A workshop is also often referred to as intensive; this may be related to its length, its specificity of focus, or both. The true work of a workshop is conducted in a small group, although often both large-group and small-group sessions are scheduled. The use of technology has a particular effect on workshop size. Finally, the folk wisdom of workshops—the generally understood, tacit knowledge of this educational format—portrays the workshop as relatively short, but examples range from forty-five-minute mini-workshops at a conference to a three-day or even three-week residential experience. The purpose and design of workshops are more helpful in distinguishing this format than exact length.

These components of a comprehensive definition of workshops are not new; neither is the need for clarity, as Sork stated so well thirteen years ago. We do have new perspectives, however, on how adults learn, on factors that affect the teaching-learning transaction, and on how to responsibly deliver meaningful programs for adults. The chapters of this sourcebook address these and other aspects of current thought and practice in adult and continuing education.

The purpose of this sourcebook is not to be a how-to manual, although authors give numerous examples, ideas, and suggestions on designing and implementing effective workshops. The real hope is that readers take this opportunity to critically examine their own work as planners, designers, facilitators, and evaluators to determine if their practice is both thoughtful and ethically responsible. This questioning and critical examination can breathe new life into this old workhorse of our profession, to keep it invigorated, responsive, and in sync with our times.

The authors of this sourcebook are all seasoned veterans of workshop planning and implementation. They respect the theoretical yet know well the realities of putting theory into practice. They have retained and built on the best practices of the past, while simultaneously filling in gaps in our awareness of teaching and learning and updating us on the contributions of workshops that are now both possible and demanded. The book begins with a look at the overall process of planning and proceeds through five chapters dealing with instructional design and delivery of workshops to an overview of evaluation processes. The two final chapters provide both a response to and a summary of the major issues presented by the authors throughout the book.

In Chapter One, Thomas J. Sork offers a synthesis of both older and newer perspectives on planning. He uses what he considers to be still-valuable contributions of "classical" planning models to create a two-dimensional framework for planning, then adds a third dimension to reflect new sensitivities and understandings of adult learning, teaching, and planning. This third dimension provides the basis for his question-based approach to planning. This approach, the means by which to activate the third dimension, also allows for adapting planning to fit the unique character of each planning situation. This chapter sets the tone for the remainder of the sourcebook and provides a context from which we can examine and come to understand how workshops are changing and becoming more complex and how adult educators are becoming more ethically responsible in working with this educational format.

An approach to workshop design based on his model of "culturally responsive teaching" is described by Raymond J. Wlodkowski in Chapter Two. He first examines the relationship of human motivation to culture. He then provides a guide to designing workshops using the four conditions of his Motivational Framework for Culturally Responsive Teaching—inclusion, attitude, meaning, and competence—to evoke and sustain intrinsic motivation and learning. Wlodkowski asserts that designing workshops with this Framework "is a way to create learning experiences where inquiry, respect, and the opportunity for full participation by diverse people is the norm."

In Chapter Three, Anne M. Will begins with distinguishing cooperative from collaborative learning, then goes on to describe the dynamics and characteristics of group learning, identifying pitfalls and giving suggestions for overcoming them. Throughout the chapter she details activities that fit the content demands and limited time frames of workshops. Will suggests that small groups promote the participant interaction and transfer of learning that distinguish effective workshops.

In the fourth chapter, Juanita Johnson-Bailey and Ronald M. Cervero draw from the literature, their own experience, and the experiences of colleagues to examine the influences of power dynamics on what is taught and learned in workshops. Rather than simply bringing these ever-present undercurrents into the realm of our awareness, they recommend ways in which workshop facilitators can successfully negotiate power relationships to result in productive learning environments, successful learning, and ethically responsible practice. Their work suggests that issues of power dynamics may be even more pronounced in workshops because of their time-limited, intense, and interactive nature.

Gretchen Bersch and I describe residential workshops in Chapter Five. We highlight the "continuous detachment" of residential programs in which participants are removed both physically and psychologically from their daily lives for an uninterrupted period of time. The results are an immersion into learning and an intensity of experience that characterize learning and living together for participants. Bersch details her experiences with adult learners and educators during residential weekends on Yukon Island near Homer, Alaska.

In Chapter Six, Chere Campbell Gibson and Terry L. Gibson review instructional technology currently being used for providing education at a distance. They go on to address issues of media selection, examine strengths and weaknesses of distance workshops, and clearly explain the need for support systems. The goal is to ensure not just access to information through technology but successful learning as well. Gibson and Gibson build on our knowledge of face-to-face learning and of technology we use every day to help us understand the new possibilities and challenges presented by distance education.

Grover J. Andrews explains in Chapter Seven that, rather than being an addendum to the process, evaluation must be an integral component in program planning. He brings to light how old myths and new wisdom about adult learners have influenced evaluation practices. He addresses reasons to evaluate, types of evaluation, and how and who evaluates, concluding with practical principles and suggestions. He includes a "Practical Guide to Assessment" developed by the International Association for Continuing Education and Training, which outlines ten different plans for customizing evaluations to fit different assessment situations.

In the eighth chapter, Doe Hentschel offers a lighthearted yet insightful and passionate look at the complex, messy, and addictive world of facilitation and workshops. Using her own experiences, she reveals, or "confesses," her perspectives on workshop planning and facilitation. From her perspective as an experienced and addicted workshop facilitator, Hentschel responds to major themes of previous chapters. She gives character and added value to this workhorse of our practice.

In the final chapter, I review the work of these authors, challenging the reader both to look at workshops with new eyes and to consider their potential for meeting current and future adult learning needs. The goal is, once again, to go beyond answering the *how-to* questions of conducting workshops and determine *how well*. These authors have given us the tools with which to do just that.

References

American Heritage Dictionary of the English Language. (3rd ed.) New York: Houghton Mifflin, 1992.

Bergevin, P., Morris, D., and Smith, R. M. *Adult Education Procedures: A Handbook of Tested Patterns for Effective Participation.* New York: Seabury Press, 1963.

Bourner, T., Martin, V., and Race, P. *Workshops That Work: 100 Ideas to Make Your Training Events More Effective.* London: McGraw-Hill, 1955.

Caffarella, R. S. *Planning Programs for Adult Learners: A Practical Guide for Educators, Trainers, and Staff Developers.* San Francisco: Jossey-Bass, 1994.

Knowles, M. S. *The Modern Practice of Adult Education: From Pedagogy to Andragogy.* Englewood Cliffs, N.J.: Prentice Hall, 1980.

Nowlen, P. M. "Program Origins." In A. B. Knox and Associates (eds.), *Developing, Administering, and Evaluating Adult Education.* San Francisco: Jossey-Bass, 1980.

Sork, T. J. "The Workshop as a Unique Instructional Format." In T. J. Sork (ed.), *Designing and Implementing Effective Workshops.* New Directions for Continuing Education, no. 22. San Francisco: Jossey-Bass, 1984.

Szcypkowski, R. S. "Objectives and Activities." In A. B. Knox and Associates (eds.), *Developing, Administering, and Evaluating Adult Education.* San Francisco: Jossey-Bass, 1980.

Jean Anderson Fleming
Editor

JEAN ANDERSON FLEMING *is assistant professor of adult and community education at Ball State University, Muncie, Indiana.*

Effective workshop planning involves melding technical know-how with social-political awareness and ethical sensitivity to produce inviting programs with a decidedly practical focus.

Workshop Planning

Thomas J. Sork

Workshops can be seductive. Those who decide to attend workshops are sometimes seduced by the promise that a great deal will be learned in a short time, by the expectation that a quick fix will be provided for a troubling or persistent problem, by the hope that a few hours or days away from work or home will renew the spirit or bolster flagging motivation, or by the prospect that interacting with others who are facing similar challenges will result in new insights or understandings. Because workshops can be seductive in many different ways, those who offer them have an obligation to address a wide range of planning issues. These include how emergent the workshop plan should be, the suitability of the workshop format, whose interests are being served by the workshop, the best way to involve people in the workshop process, and the predictability of outcomes. The latter concern dictates what claims should be made about how the program will benefit participants.

Seducing adult learners into programs might be regarded by some as a respectable, even an honorable, activity, whereas others might regard it as irresponsible or immoral. This chapter provides a framework for educational design that encourages a thoughtful, responsible approach to planning. This approach integrates the best of what Cervero and Wilson (1994) call "classical" planning models with new sensitivities and understandings about planning, education, and learning to produce workshops that no one will mind being seduced into attending.

This chapter begins with a review of the evolution of planning theory, proceeds with a summary of the still-useful contributions made by classical planning models, then moves to a discussion of new sensitivities and understandings that have important implications for planning workshops. The chapter ends with a description of a question-based approach to planning

New Directions for Adult and Continuing Education, no. 76, Winter 1997 © Jossey-Bass Publishers

workshops that overcomes the limitations of classical models and acknowledges the unique character of every planning situation.

Evolution of Planning Theory

It is undeniable that classical, rational planning models have dominated thinking and writing about program planning for nearly half a century. Early works of Ralph Tyler (1949) and Malcolm Knowles (1950) influenced generations of educational theorists. The perspectives on educational planning Tyler and Knowles developed were attractive because they shifted focus from the teacher to the learner. They proposed systematic approaches to meeting educational needs of learners while encouraging accountability through the use of outcome-oriented objectives and systematic evaluation. These innovations were consistent with the progressive education movement of the time and with the influential philosophy of John Dewey.

Tyler was interested in public schooling, whereas Knowles was interested in informal adult education, so for these writers the types of learners and the settings for learning were different. Nevertheless, each of these men proposed frameworks for thinking about educational planning that gained many supporters, including those who subsequently wrote about planning adult education programs. Although early critics found weaknesses in both frameworks, the criticisms did not prevent widespread adoption of both Tylerian and Knowlesian approaches to planning.

Of the dozens of books written about program planning since the 1950s, few have departed significantly from the classical, rational model. Even the innovative approach of Paulo Freire (1970) that focused on helping people recognize and struggle against oppression can be viewed as a variation of classical, rational planning models.

More recently, concerns have been raised about the degree to which classical models reflect what practitioners actually do and how well they identify the most important issues to consider as programs are planned. Cervero and Wilson (1994, 1996), for example, argue that most models focus almost exclusively on the technical aspects of planning and largely ignore the "people work"—the messy, unpredictable, social-political dynamics that unfold during the process. Cervero and Wilson view planning as a process of negotiation among people with different interests and power relations. Planners are urged to "read" the situations they confront and to adopt strategies that promote responsible planning characterized by democratic participation, political awareness, and ethical sensitivity. Their framework for planning recognizes the enduring contributions of classical planning models while emphasizing the often-ignored human dynamics of planning. The case studies they provide do a good job of illustrating the extent to which personal interests influence planning and of identifying strategies planners often use to deal with asymmetrical power relations among stakeholders.

Caffarella (1994) presents a nonlinear and highly practical model that reflects the influence of Houle (1972, 1996) and others in its language and structure but that has a unique focus on the application and transfer of learning. She uses the work of Ottoson (1993, 1994, 1997) and others who have studied issues related to application and transfer of learning to encourage planners to incorporate strategies that are likely to promote changes in practice when learners return to their natural environments: the home, family, workplace, community, and so on. This concern with application is not new in adult education, but it seems to be enjoying renewed emphasis. Because workshops are typically designed to help participants respond to some immediate concern or issue, strategies for application become central to their planning.

Contributions from Classical, Rational Models

Imbedded in classical planning models are several enduring principles that continue to influence both theorists and practitioners. Although there have been debates about the details of some of these principles, they remain important considerations for planning any type of adult education program. Following is a brief summary of principles that I regard as particularly relevant to workshop planning.

Honoring the Learner's Experience, Perspective, and Expectations. Knowles (1970) is generally credited with popularizing the concept of andragogy in North America. Although I regard his assumptions about adult learners as overly romantic and mildly paternalistic, he presents a compelling argument in support of learner-centered planning. The tenets of andragogy place the interests of learners above those of either educators or institutions. I fear, however, that learner-centered planning is sometimes used by educators as an excuse to avoid making difficult decisions.

Recognizing the Importance of Diversity. Within the past fifteen years in particular, there has been increasing concern with diversity and difference and their implications for adult learning and education. Few planning models refer explicitly to diversity, but it is clear to me that responsible practice must be sensitive to diversity in its many forms. Gender, race, ethnicity, and class remain central concerns, but other forms of diversity—including sexual orientation, linguistic background, religious orientation, ability or disability, and so on—represent differences with implications for workshop planning. The exact nature of these implications is not always evident without careful analysis, but planners who ignore them do so at their peril. (In Chapter Four, Johnson-Bailey and Cervero examine the influences of power relationships on learning in depth.)

Involving Stakeholders in Planning. Conventional wisdom holds that adults should always be involved in planning programs in which they participate, yet most of the adult educators I ask admit they rarely involve learners or other stakeholders substantively in planning. The recent case studies of planning found in Cervero and Wilson (1996) confirm an uneven application of this tenet. Indeed, some of the cases illustrate how deliberately excluding stakeholders from planning is used as a strategy for giving voice to those in less-powerful positions. The moral arguments that support such practices will be acceptable to some but rejected by others. (Andrews discusses involving stakeholders in the planning process and in the development of evaluation plans in Chapter Seven.)

Understanding the Importance of the Context in Which Planning Occurs. The context—social, economic, cultural, political, organizational—of planning has long been regarded as important. What is less clear, however, is which specific features of the context are important to consider in the planning process.

Basing Programs on the Needs of Learners. This is another manifestation of learner-centered education and has become a standard feature of classical models. But as will be discussed later, needs-based planning is inherently reactive and therefore has limitations in the rapidly changing circumstances of the late twentieth century. Although needs assessment remains an important planning tool, it is dangerous to assume that it is always the correct tool to use. When leading workshops on needs assessment during the past few years, I have found myself advising participants against doing them when other strategies seemed more promising. Several of these other strategies will be identified in the concluding section of this chapter.

Clarifying the Aims or Goals of the Workshop. Developing objectives has persisted as an element in most classical planning models despite compelling criticisms leveled against the "objectives movement." As with needs assessment, objectives are a powerful planning tool when used in the right circumstances for the right purpose. But objectives are often not the best tool with which to clarify what it is we hope will happen as a result of programs. Alternatives to objectives, such as descriptions of purposes, processes, benefits, and content are less precise than objectives, but they also require much less effort and do suggest outcomes, although indirectly.

Incorporating Workshop Processes That Actively Involve Learners. Workshops are, by definition, active learning environments where participants expect hands-on practice and a high degree of interaction and collaborative learning. There is nothing more deadly than to create these expectations by calling a program a "workshop" and then delivering an experience that is didactic, nonparticipatory, and not focused on the immediate needs of learners. (In Chapter Three, Will presents numerous small-group work activities and strategies.)

Choosing Facilitators or Instructors and Instructional Resources with Great Care. The interpersonal dynamics of workshops can be a challenge to manage. The study reported by Lewis and Dunlop (1991) confirmed the important role instructors play in the success or failure of programs. Workshop facilitators must possess not only the skills necessary to engage people in the learning task but also the personality characteristics and sensitivities that allow them to respond appropriately to unpredictable process issues such as conflict, confusion, and communication problems. Other resources, such as physical space, films or videos, and print materials, must also be selected with sensitivity to issues such as inclusiveness and accessibility.

Promoting Application of Learning as a Central Theme. Because learners expect workshops to be immediately helpful in some way, attending carefully to issues of application of learning in planning is vital. Workshops can be designed to enhance the prospect that what is learned will be applied in the learner's natural environment, but it is not always clear which design elements will be most effective in promoting that application. (In Chapter Two, Wlodkowski presents a framework for workshop design to keep intrinsic motivation, learning, and transfer high.)

Attending Carefully to Administrative Details. I have seen otherwise well-planned and executed workshops fail because of administrative oversights that annoyed participants, disrupted the schedule, interfered with group process, or distracted everyone from the task. We often concentrate so hard on the instructional aspects of the program that we forget to attend to the myriad administrative details that are equally instrumental to success.

Caring for the Physical and Emotional Needs of Workshop Participants. The intensity of workshops can magnify the effects of stress and fatigue on participants. Interpersonal dynamics and differences combined with stress, fatigue, time constraints, and other contributing factors can lead to participants disengaging from the program physically, intellectually, and emotionally. Workshop planners who are sensitive to these matters can incorporate design elements such as carefully timed breaks, debriefing sessions, periodic check-backs, and other strategies to both relieve stress and provide facilitators an opportunity to monitor the physical and emotional condition of participants.

Assessing Program Outcomes in Addition to Learner Satisfaction. Cervero (1984), along with many other authors, has encouraged the evaluation of more than the satisfaction of participants. Satisfaction is often considered a desirable outcome of workshops, but focusing exclusively on satisfaction in evaluation is a problem. The assumptions that *satisfied* participants must have learned something of value and that *unsatisfied* participants must not have learned something of value are suspect because there are good counterexamples of each. If our primary objective is to make people happy, then we are in the wrong line of work.

New Sensitivities and Understandings

Recent work in adult education has been influenced by various movements and theoretical perspectives that come from outside the field. These include feminism, postmodernism, critical theory, and multiculturalism, among many others. Each of these has spawned concerns about the provision of education and has implications for how we plan programs. Each of these is discussed here briefly, including some tentative thoughts on their implications for workshop design.

Feminisms. The plural is used here because there are many varieties of feminism, each of which has a somewhat different focus. What the varieties have in common is a concern with gender and power. Critical feminist analyses of adult education theory have revealed serious weaknesses in some long-held views about adult development, learning styles, and preferences and the distortions created by essentializing either men or women as learners. The work by Goldberger, Tarule, Clinchy, and Belenky (1996) and Stalker (1996), for example, challenges gender-insensitive theories about adult learning. Other detailed studies of women learners should shake our confidence in what we think we know about women's learning (MacKeracher, 1993; Chapman, 1996). Gender does make a difference in learning, and this should be taken into account in planning.

Postmodernism. Like feminism, there are many versions of postmodernism, each of which challenges metanarratives that attempt to describe or explain an objective reality divorced from context and social processes. Postmodern analysis raises disturbing questions about planning. Plans are a product of someone's understanding of which educative experiences will produce which outcomes. The veracity of cause-effect relationships that are not the product of contextualized, socially situated knowledge construction are suspect in a postmodern world. The postmodern perspective challenges planners to recognize the limitations of technicist approaches to education and the dangers of practicing while unaware of the ideological and cultural forces that influence actions (Briton, 1996). Planners are further challenged to create designs that encourage and respect the variety of perspectives on what knowledge is legitimate and how knowledge can be constructed or reconstructed as part of the educational process.

Critical Theory. Critical theory is concerned with power, its manifestations, and its effects. As the late Paulo Freire (1985) and many others have argued, education is a political act that involves the exercise of power. Planning involves the exercise of power to further personal and organizational interests. Cervero and Wilson (1994, 1996) regard planning as a process of negotiating interests among people with varying power relations. Very often these power relations are dramatically asymmetrical, meaning that the parties involved in planning have unequal power. This framework for thinking about workshop planning helps sensitize us to our own power (which Cervero and Wilson define as the enduring ability to act), specifically to how power can be used and abused as we pursue our interests through education and how our own power relates to the power of other stakeholders.

Multiculturalism. Culture is one form of difference that has received a great deal of attention in recent years. Like gender, cultural differences are often not adequately addressed in educational planning. Although it is dangerous to generalize too broadly about characteristics of various cultural groups and their educational implications, we do know that culture makes a difference in how people communicate, how they participate in programs, how they regard facilitators and others who might be regarded as "experts," and how they relate to people from other cultures. It is not enough to recognize and respect these differences; educational planners must be able to design workshops that fully engage people in learning who might have very different cultural traditions and expectations. This demands not only an awareness of cultural differences but also the ability to adapt the design so that it encourages full participation and active learning by all those attending (Martin, 1993). (Wlodkowski in Chapter Two presents a framework for culturally responsive teaching to ensure the inclusion of diverse people.)

Question-Based Approach to Workshop Planning

A vexing problem when presenting either a visual or verbal summary of any complex process, in this case planning, is that summaries can never include all important aspects of planning and the unpredictable, interactive character of planning in practice. And yet such summaries are useful reminders of key concepts and processes that can assist planners. In my own teaching I use a diagram (see Figure 1.1) that I continually revise as my thoughts about planning change and I receive feedback from students. This diagram represents the major *processes* involved in educational planning, but, as will be explained below, this two-dimensional representation conceals complex aspects of planning that are often ignored in the literature and overlooked in practice. Each element requires a bit of explanation. Following a discussion of each of these process elements, I explain this hidden but very important third dimension of planning. The six elements are clustered around a core of formative evaluation, indicating that constant assessment of the quality of the plan and a willingness to reconsider and revise the plan are central to responsible planning.

Figure 1.1. Basic Elements of Program Planning

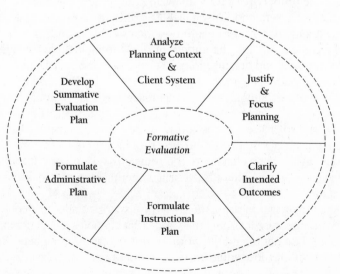

In addition to using a three-dimensional planning model, I have also moved to what I call a question-based approach to educational design that avoids prescribing that planning should be done in a certain way. Each planning situation is sufficiently unique that it is impossible—and irresponsible—to suggest that a particular approach to planning is applicable to all or most workshop planning situations. Instead, I believe planners should take a question-posing stance in which they reflect on the key questions that must be asked and answered during planning to arrive at an appropriate design. These questions are associated with different layers of the third dimension. As will be discussed later in that section, some of these questions will be technical in character and can be answered using common planning tools. Other questions deal with the social-political or ethical aspects of planning. Answering these questions requires an ability to be critically self-reflective and a willingness to confront issues related to power and ethics.

Elements of Planning

All planning models contain elements or clusters of tasks that are regarded as important when designing programs. Figure 1.1 presents six basic elements of program planning, each of which addresses a crucial aspect of workshop design. These elements have their origins in classical models, but I have adapted them to my own way of thinking about planning and to overcome some of the weaknesses in conventional approaches.

Analyze Planning Context and Client System. This element of planning is not made explicit in many models, but it is an integral part of the process. The context of planning is the milieu or setting in which it occurs. Understanding the factors and forces that are important to consider in the process is the primary reason for analyzing the context (Sork and Caffarella, 1989). But as Cervero and Wilson (1994) point out, the planner also acts on the context and changes it as planning progresses. The kinds of information about the context that may be important in planning include the mission or aims of the groups and organizations involved; political, social, and economic forces; how the sponsors of the program are regarded by those in the client group; the accountability framework that reflects who is accountable to whom and for what; frame factors that determine the latitude that planners perceive they have; and so on. Being consciously aware of these elements of context as planning progresses is important because they have an influence on our plans. If we are unaware of an element of the context that is important to planning our workshop, we may find ourselves encountering barriers, blocks, or missed opportunities.

There is a danger in using the term *client system* to refer to a collective of adult learners because for some the word *client* connotes a dependent role or relationship. I do not intend the word to convey that meaning here. Instead I use it as a label for those adult learners who we hope might be attracted to a particular workshop. Other terms that are used to refer to this collective of learners include *target group* and *customers,* but I do not find either of these any less objectionable than *client.*

The client system is not the same as *participants* because participants are usually a subset of the client system. For planning any program, the boundaries of the client system are defined in varying degrees of detail. Sometimes the boundary between clients and nonclients is clear and nonnegotiable, as in the case of a workshop designed for employees of an organization. In this example the planner would likely know a great deal about the clients, including their age, gender, race or ethnicity, educational background, work experience, where they live, discretionary time, and so on. In other cases the boundary can be fuzzy and open to interpretation, as in the case of workshops designed for the community or for any adult learners with an interest in the topic. In this example we might know very little about the clients other than that they are adults who live in a particular jurisdiction. The biggest challenges in analyzing the client system are drawing the clearest boundaries possible between clients and nonclients and gathering information about the clients that may be important to the success of the workshop.

Justify and Focus Planning. In conventional planning models this element would be labeled *assess needs.* I have dropped that term from my model because I regard needs assessment as only one of several means to justify and focus the planning of workshops. Basing programs on needs of adult learners—when needs are thought of as gaps between present and desired abilities—is also a reactive rather than a proactive approach to planning, because a need cannot be identified until an undesirable gap exists. Given what I see happening to the planet and to oppressed people around the world, I do not believe that the end of the twentieth century is a safe time to be working in an occupation that is primarily reactive (some prefer *responsive*) to the needs of adult learners. Needs assessment remains a powerful tool for planning, but when done well it requires substantial time and other limited resources. Other approaches to justify and focus planning are interest inventories, problem analyses, trend analyses, and market testing (Sork, 1987). These alternatives require less time and resources yet still can produce all the information needed to plan the program.

Clarify Intended Outcomes. Until a few years ago I referred to this element as *develop objectives,* but I changed it in recognition of the many different ways that planners clarify intended outcomes, both explicitly and implicitly. Clarifying what we hope will be achieved in workshops is still regarded as a necessary element of planning. Developing a set of objectives is a powerful way to clarify intentions, but it is neither the only nor necessarily the best way (Sork, 1997). We often sufficiently clarify intentions by describing purposes of programs, listing benefits, explaining the educational process involved, and so on. Sometimes we wish to make outcomes explicit; other times outcomes will be emergent and it would be foolhardy to make them explicit during planning.

Formulate Instructional Plan. Instructional planning is often where we begin because it is the substance of the program and the domain where our creativity and expertise are best applied. It is here where decisions are made about the structure of the program, the instructional resources that will be used, the sequencing of events, how the facilitator will relate to the participants, how motivation will be maintained, and so on. Information about the clients becomes particularly relevant during instructional planning because the decisions made here should reflect such characteristics as gender, cultural background, education, facility with language, abilities or disabilities, and so on.

Formulate Administrative Plan. Administrative planning includes marketing or advertising the program, attending to financial matters, and identifying and scheduling the myriad tasks that must be completed before, during, and after the program. These matters have an important bearing on program success. For example, how the workshop is marketed to the client system creates expectations among prospective participants. Fees charged must be carefully calculated to cover costs but also to be consistent with the clients' willingness and ability to pay. All key tasks must be scheduled so that they are completed on time and in the necessary sequence.

Develop Summative Evaluation Plan. Summative evaluation involves making judgments about the value of a program by gathering evidence related to program outcomes and comparing that evidence to expectations (Steele, 1975). Formative evaluation, on the other hand, is something that occurs throughout planning and involves reviewing plans as they are developed and making improvements to those plans before they are implemented. Summative evaluation plans can focus on one or more levels of evaluation (Kirkpatrick, 1987), from reactions (satisfaction), to learning outcomes, to application of learning, through the results of application of learning. (In Chapter Seven, Andrews treats evaluation and assessment in depth.)

The Third Dimension of Workshop Planning

A key limitation of all two-dimensional planning models is that they do not address the complex range of issues that might be confronted by workshop planners. For example, Figure 1.1 is a typical two-dimensional planning model that includes common elements found in other models, but because it is two-dimensional it does not prompt planners to consider more than the technical, how-to aspects of planning. Figure 1.2 represents the third dimension of planning that is hidden in Figure 1.1. This third dimension is important when planning workshops and other types of programs because it recognizes that other concerns lurk below the technical level.

Technical. The technical aspects of planning are at the surface of the planning process. Because they are on the surface, they have received the most attention and are often the ones of greatest concern to practitioners. Skilled planners are knowledgeable about a wide range of technical planning tools available to them and know when to use each tool. Unfortunately, a preoccupation with the technical aspects of planning has distracted us from deeper, and equally important, levels (Cervero and Wilson, 1994; Sork, 1996).

Figure 1.2. The Third Dimension of Workshop Planning

Surface

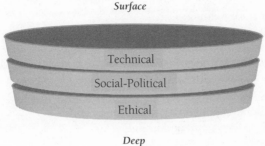

Deep

Social-Political. The interplay of power and interests in planning and the complexities of involving other people in the process are the essence of this level of planning. The social-political layer applies to each of the six elements of planning. In other words, there are social-political dimensions to analyzing the planning context and client system, to justifying and focusing planning, to clarifying intended outcomes, and so on.

Ethical. This is the deepest level of planning and, I fear, the one least often considered. Concerns about the ethical aspects of planning are not new (Singarella and Sork, 1983; Sork, 1988; Cervero and Wilson, 1994), but I have yet to find a planning model that makes them a central feature. This level is about being aware of the *ethical content* of our work and recognizing when we should be reflecting on and discussing the moral justification for what we are doing or not doing. Who is included and excluded from the client system and why is a question that begs for discussion. Answering the *why* question may reveal moral arguments that should be subjected to critical analysis. Are the reasons for including or excluding certain people or groups justifiable on moral grounds? Each of the six elements of planning has ethical content, but it is impossible to pose a set of questions that will apply to all planning situations. The important point is that skilled planners should recognize when it is necessary to pose a question related to the ethics of planning and then know how to arrive at a satisfactory answer.

Concluding Comments

This chapter contains some ideas about workshop planning that were not part of conventional wisdom when the first sourcebook on this topic was published (Sork, 1984). Since that time we have recognized the limits of classical planning models and have become more sensitive to a wide range of issues relevant to our practice. The third dimension of planning is the way I have incorporated these issues into my own planning model. Moving to the question-based approach to planning as represented by this third dimension provides greater freedom to those who recognize that every planning situation is unique and that no model can adequately anticipate the complexities and challenges a workshop planner will face in any given circumstance. A broad and flexible framework, such as the one presented here, can be a helpful tool to guide the work of planners.

Educational planning remains one of the most critical aspects of adult and continuing education because it is through programs that learners and learning resources are brought together. How effective programs are depends in part on the skills and sensitivities of planners. In the following chapters you will find more ideas and advice about designing and implementing effective workshops. Using them responsibly will produce workshops that no one will be sorry they were seduced into attending.

References

Briton, D. *The Modern Practice of Adult Education: A Postmodern Critique.* Albany: State University of New York Press, 1996.

Caffarella, R. S. *Planning Programs for Adult Learners: A Practical Guide for Educators, Trainers and Staff Developers.* San Francisco: Jossey-Bass, 1994.

Cervero, R. M. "Evaluating Workshop Implementation and Outcomes." In T. J. Sork (ed.), *Designing and Implementing Effective Workshops.* New Directions for Adult and Continuing Education, no. 22. San Francisco: Jossey-Bass, 1984.

Cervero, R. M., and Wilson, A. L. *Planning Responsibly for Adult Education: A Guide to Negotiating Power and Interests.* San Francisco: Jossey-Bass, 1994.

Cervero, R. M., and Wilson, A. L. (eds.). *What Really Matters in Adult Education Program Planning: Lessons in Negotiating Power and Interests.* New Directions for Adult and Continuing Education, no. 69. San Francisco: Jossey-Bass, 1996.

Chapman, V. L. "All This Talk: Stories of Women Learning." In *Proceedings of the Annual Conference of the Canadian Association for the Study of Adult Education.* Winnipeg: University of Manitoba, 1996.

Freire, P. *Pedagogy of the Oppressed.* New York: Herder and Herder, 1970.

Freire, P. *The Politics of Education: Culture, Power and Liberation.* South Hadley, Mass.: Bergin and Garvey, 1985.

Goldberger, N. R., Tarule, J. M., Clinchy, B. M., and Belenky, M. F. (eds.). *Knowledge, Difference and Power: Essays Inspired by Women's Ways of Knowing.* New York: Basic Books, 1996.

Houle, C. O. *The Design of Education.* San Francisco: Jossey-Bass, 1972.

Houle, C. O. *The Design of Education.* (2nd ed.) San Francisco: Jossey-Bass, 1996.

Kirkpatrick, D. L. "Evaluation." In R. L. Craig (ed.), *Training and Development Handbook.* (3rd ed.) New York: McGraw-Hill, 1987.

Knowles, M. S. *Informal Adult Education.* New York: Association Press, 1950.

Knowles, M. S. *The Modern Practice of Adult Education: Andragogy vs. Pedagogy.* New York: Association Press, 1970.

Lewis, C. H., and Dunlop, C. C. "Successful and Unsuccessful Adult Education Programs: Perceptions, Explanations and Implications." In T. J. Sork (ed.), *Mistakes Made and Lessons Learned: Overcoming Obstacles to Successful Program Planning.* New Directions for Adult and Continuing Education, no. 49. San Francisco: Jossey-Bass, 1991.

MacKeracher, D. "Women as Learners." In T. Barer-Stein and J. A. Draper (eds.), *The Craft of Teaching Adults.* (2nd ed.) Toronto: Culture Concepts, 1993.

Martin, P. "Considerations for Aboriginal Adult Education Program Planning." *Canadian Journal of Native Education,* 1993, *20* (1), 168–175.

Ottoson, J. M. "Implementation Research: Understanding the Application of Learning Following Continuing Professional Education." In D. Flannery (ed.), *Proceedings of the 34th*

Annual Adult Education Research Conference. University Park: Pennsylvania State University, 1993.

Ottoson, J. M. "Transfer of Learning: Not Just an Afterthought." *Adult Learning,* 1994, 5 (4), 21.

Ottoson, J. M. "After the Applause: Exploring Multiple Influences on Application Following an Adult Education Program." *Adult Education Quarterly,* 1997, 47 (2), 92–107.

Singarella, T. A., and Sork, T. J. "Questions of Value and Conduct: Ethical Issues for Adult Education." *Adult Education Quarterly,* 1983, 33 (4), 244–251.

Sork, T. J. (ed.). *Designing and Implementing Effective Workshops.* New Directions for Adult and Continuing Education, no. 22. San Francisco: Jossey-Bass, 1984.

Sork, T. J. "Needs Assessment as Part of Program Planning." In Q. H. Gessner (ed.), *Handbook of Continuing Higher Education.* New York: American Council on Education/Macmillan, 1987.

Sork, T. J. "Ethical Issues in Program Planning." In R. G. Brockett (ed.), *Ethical Issues in Adult Education.* New York: Teachers College Press, 1988.

Sork, T. J. "Negotiating Power and Interests in Planning: A Critical Perspective." In R. M. Cervero and A. L. Wilson (eds.), *What Really Matters in Adult Education Program Planning: Lessons in Negotiating Power and Interests.* New Directions for Adult and Continuing Education, no. 69. San Francisco: Jossey-Bass, 1996.

Sork, T. J. "Program Priorities, Purposes and Objectives." In P. S. Cookson (ed.), *Program Planning for the Training and Education of Adults: North American Perspectives.* Malabar, Fla.: Krieger, 1997.

Sork, T. J., and Caffarella, R. S. "Planning Programs for Adults." In S. B. Merriam and P. M. Cunningham (eds.), *Handbook of Adult and Continuing Education.* San Francisco: Jossey-Bass, 1989.

Stalker, J. "Women and Adult Education Research: Rethinking Androcentric Research." *Adult Education Quarterly,* 1996, 46 (2), 98–113.

Steele, S. M. "An Emerging Concept of Program Evaluation." *Journal of Extension,* 1975, 13, 13–22.

Tyler, R. W. *Basic Principles of Curriculum and Instruction.* Chicago: University of Chicago Press, 1949.

THOMAS J. SORK is a faculty member in the adult education program at the University of British Columbia and is spending more time these days in the third dimension of planning.

Human motivation is inseparable from culture. The Motivational Framework for Culturally Responsive Teaching is presented as a guide for designing effective workshops for all participants.

Motivation with a Mission: Understanding Motivation and Culture in Workshop Design

Raymond J. Wlodkowski

It is early Saturday morning. The thirty adults filing into your classroom are strangers to you. You are aware that they are required to be there. Their apparent weariness rolls off them like fog descending a darkened hill. You are the workshop leader and you know you must remain buoyant. You remind yourself, "This is a challenge I wanted. I've done this before and it's turned out well." You are not quite sure if you are a bit anxious, a bit excited, or simply charged to ward off your own fatigue. But one thing you are certain of: you better have a good workshop plan and you better get off to a good start. This does not look like a group that will easily forgive.

For most workshop leaders, this scenario is probably more threatening and dismal than the norm. Yet anyone who conducts workshops on a regular basis usually faces one or more of these elements. Perhaps it is an inopportune time for learning, unfamiliar faces or places, or the exhaustion from a long day's schedule. Often, however, there is a saving grace: participants earnestly believe that they need the workshop. This feeling of necessity is the genesis for the workshop and its impetus. Participants usually come to learn something that they or someone else believes to be important. It may be to solve a problem, to learn a skill, or to become aware of newly developing technology. This is crucial because when adults do not feel a need to learn, an otherwise effective workshop has the possibility of ranging from a palpable challenge to an embarrassing fiasco. A *well-designed* workshop can dramatically increase the odds that it will summon learning rather than humiliation.

The foundation for workshop design that follows is based on a comprehensive model of *culturally responsive teaching,* a pedagogy that crosses disciplines and cultures to respectfully engage all learners (Wlodkowski and Ginsberg, 1995). This particular approach reflects the value of human motivation and the principle that motivation is inseparable from culture. Its basis lies in theories of intrinsic motivation. The major goal of this approach to workshop design is to create a learning experience that evokes the intrinsic motivation of participants throughout the workshop and encourages them to use what they have learned.

This chapter proceeds with an overview of the relationship of motivation to culture and the Motivational Framework for Culturally Responsive Teaching (Wlodkowski and Ginsberg, 1995). It offers a guide to designing workshops that includes clarifying the workshop's purpose, understanding participants' perspectives and knowledge, and using the four motivational conditions of the framework—inclusion, attitude, meaning, and competence—to create a workshop. The chapter ends with an example of a completely designed workshop that highlights transfer of learning to the workplace.

Motivation Is Inseparable from Culture

Increasingly, workshops are multicultural environments where teachers must relate the content to the various cultural backgrounds of their learners. Teaching that ignores or trivializes learners' norms of behavior and communication provokes resistance.

Engagement in learning is the visible outcome of motivation, the natural capacity to direct energy in the pursuit of a goal. Our emotions influence our motivation. In turn, our emotions are socialized through culture—the deeply learned confluence of language, beliefs, values, and behaviors that pervades every aspect of our lives. What may elicit frustration, joy, or determination may differ across cultures, because cultures differ in their definitions of novelty, intimacy, opportunity, and gratification and in their definitions of appropriate responses (Kitayama and Markus, 1994). For example, many workshops begin with ice-breakers, activities where, on occasion, learners may be asked to self-disclose personal feelings or circumstances to strangers, such as incidents that significantly changed his or her life or moments when he or she felt passionate about something. Some people enjoy sharing such personal information with people who are relatively unknown to them. However, studies consistently reveal that self-disclosure of this nature may be incompatible with the cultural values of Asian Americans, Latinos, and American Indians, who often reserve expression of personal feelings for the intimacy of family (Sue and Sue, 1990). An early request for self-disclosure might be disconcerting for people from these ethnic backgrounds.

The Motivational Framework for Culturally Responsive Teaching

From the perspective of intrinsic motivation, it is part of human nature to be curious, to be active, to initiate thought and behavior, to make meaning from experience, and to be effective at what we value. These primary sources of motivation reside in all of us, across all cultures. When learners can see that what they are learning makes sense and is important, their intrinsic motivation emerges. Theories of intrinsic motivation have been successfully applied and researched in areas such as cross-cultural studies and adult learning (Wlodkowski, 1985; Csikszentmihalyi and Csikszentmihalyi, 1988) and education, work, and sports (Deci and Ryan, 1985). With intrinsic motivation as the foundation for learning, the learner's perspective is central to teaching.

In the case of extrinsic motivation, the teaching focus is on the use of extrinsic rewards such as grades, money, and status to reinforce learning. The learners' perspective is not the fundamental motivational consideration. However, as both practitioners and researchers attest, when extrinsic rewards continue to be the primary motivators, intrinsic motivation is dampened (Deci and Ryan, 1991; Wlodkowski and Ginsberg, 1995). Those learners whose socialization accommodates the extrinsic approach surge ahead, while those learners—often the marginalized—whose socialization does not, fall behind. To promote equitable learning among *all* learners, a holistic, culturally responsive pedagogy based on intrinsic motivation is needed. This is especially so when what is learned at a workshop may be critical to the continuing employment and advancement of the adult learners.

The Motivational Framework for Culturally Responsive Teaching is respectful of different cultures and is capable of creating a common culture within a learning situation that all learners can accept. In this model, pedagogical alignment—the coordination of approaches to teaching that ensure maximum consistent effect—is critical. The more harmonious the elements of the workshop design are, the more likely they are to evoke, encourage, and sustain intrinsic motivation.

This framework includes four motivational conditions that the teacher and learners continuously create or enhance:

1. *Establishing inclusion:* creating a learning atmosphere in which learners and teachers feel respected by and connected to one another.
2. *Developing attitude:* creating a favorable disposition toward the learning experience through personal relevance and choice.
3. *Enhancing meaning:* creating challenging, thoughtful learning experiences that include learners' perspectives and values.
4. *Engendering competence:* creating an understanding that learners are effective in learning something they value.

These conditions are essential for developing intrinsic motivation among all learners throughout a workshop or other conventional learning experiences such as college courses and training programs. These motivational conditions work in concert as they influence teachers and learners, and they happen in a moment as well as over a period of time. The workshop leader must plan how to establish and coordinate the conditions. A good place to begin is to be clear about the purpose of the workshop. Equally important is gaining an understanding of the participants. Both of these considerations are essential to crafting the four conditions into an excellent workshop. (In Chapter One, Sork pays particular attention to these principles in his overview of the planning process.)

Clarifying the Purpose of the Workshop

As soon as participants know the objectives and procedures of a workshop, they begin to form a personal theory about the choices and competencies necessary for accomplishing those tasks. Clearly defined objectives can heighten participants' conscious awareness of personal control and competence. Confusion is less likely, and the learners can more clearly understand and discuss what is expected of them. For nonnative speakers of English, this may be critical. Because most workshops have a mission to develop applied knowledge and skills, learning objectives offer a way to state what learners are likely to know, do, or feel as a result of the workshop.

Entire books have been written about how to construct learning objectives. The three essential elements are a statement of *who* (the learners), *how* (the action verb), and *what* (the content), for example: "As a result of this workshop, participants (the learners) will construct (the action verb) a résumé containing their professional achievements (the content)." Once the learning objectives for the workshop are determined, the teacher is in a much better position to select content material and to create a cohesively designed program that establishes the four conditions of the Motivational Framework for Culturally Responsive Teaching. However, we should not feel compelled to abandon those educational aims that cannot be reduced to measurable forms of predictable performance. Often we conduct workshops to solve problems without predetermining the outcomes, as when a consultant conducts a workshop to address communication problems in a particular work setting.

Understanding Workshop Participants' Knowledge, Skills, and Perspectives

Critical to the design of a motivating and culturally responsive workshop is a respectful understanding of the knowledge, skills, and especially the perspectives and concerns of participants. There may be conflict with management, anticipated downsizing, resistance to a new technology, racial tension, or a new administration, to name just a few of the possibilities that could influence the attitudes of participants toward the workshop. Or it is possible that the participants may be a very cohesive group, highly motivated to learn the content of the workshop; spending time to establish inclusion would be unnecessarily frustrating for the teacher as well as the learners. In any of these cases, a perceptive awareness of workshop participants is indispensable to designing an excellent workshop. Methods for better understanding participants can range from visiting the workplace, to interviews, to written surveys.

Designing the Workshop from a Motivational Perspective: Guiding Questions and Strategies

Because most workshops have specific learning objectives, they tend to be linear and prescriptive: teachers sequence learning events over time and predetermine the order in which concepts and skills are taught and when they are practiced and applied. Although human motivation is not tidy, one can plan ways to evoke it throughout a learning sequence. In fact, because of motivation's emotional base and natural instability, it is wise, especially with a limited time period for learning, to painstakingly arrange and create the milieu and learning activities that can enhance adult motivation. In this manner, we do not "motivate" participants but create with them opportunities, experiences, and environments more likely to elicit their intrinsic motivation.

Questions.   One way to begin is for the instructor to take the four motivational conditions from the framework and transpose them into questions to use as guidelines for selecting motivational strategies and learning activities for the workshop.

1. Establishing inclusion: How do I create or affirm a learning atmosphere in which the participants feel respected and connected? (This is best planned for the beginning of the workshop.)
2. Developing attitude: How do I create or affirm a favorable disposition toward learning through personal relevance and choice? (This is best planned for the beginning of the workshop.)
3. Enhancing meaning: How do I create engaging and challenging learning experiences that include learner perspectives and values? (This is best planned for throughout the workshop.)
4. Engendering competence: How do I create or affirm an understanding that participants have effectively learned something they value and perceive as authentic to their real world? (This is best planned for the ending of the workshop.)

Strategies.   A motivational strategy is a deliberate teacher action or instructional process that is likely to enhance the participant's motivation to learn (Wlodkowski, 1985). For example, *to provide variety in the processes and materials used for learning* is a motivational strategy. People are naturally curious and tend to pay more attention to things that are changing than to things that are unchanging. Variety is stimulating and draws learner interest toward its source. Therefore a teacher could *change* methods of instruction (from discussion to a game) or materials (from looking at pictures in a book to looking at a video) to evoke more learner interest.

Although there are numerous motivational strategies (Wlodkowski, 1985; Wlodkowski and Ginsberg, 1995), the briefness of this chapter allows for the explication of only a few. The following strategies have been selected because they are generally effective within and across cultures and because they are very useful with adults. They are well documented in the literature of multicultural education as well as adult learning. These strategies are categorized according to the motivational condition to which they most directly contribute.

Establishing Inclusion. Feelings of cultural isolation can deteriorate adult motivation to learn. When the workshop leader sets a tone that the integrity of each person is valued, the expression of each learner's perspective is welcomed. In a *climate of respect,* intrinsic motivation can emerge because people can be authentic and spontaneous, voicing relevant matters. *Feeling connected* to the learning group also draws forth intrinsic motivation because social needs are met and people can feel free enough to risk the mistakes that true learning involves and to share their resources and strengths. Described next are two important strategies that enhance respect and connection.

Multidimensional sharing occurs on those occasions, from introduction exercises to social activities, when people have a better chance to see one another as complete and evolving human beings who have mutual needs, emotions, and experiences. These opportunities give a human face to the workshop, help break down stereotypes, and support the identification of the self in the realm of another person's world. As introductory activities, these are usually most inclusive and motivating when they help people learn each other's names, validate the unique experience of the individuals involved, and relieve the normal tension that most new groups feel in the beginning of a workshop. The following safe and basic example can be used as a small or large group process. Each person introduces herself or himself, names one to five of the places he or she has lived, and offers one expectation, concern, or hope that he or she has for the workshop. The range of possibilities for multidimensional sharing is enormous. The caution is to be more subtle than intrusive.

Collaborative learning includes the variety of educational approaches involving joint intellectual efforts by learners or by learners and teachers together. In these situations, participants are working in groups of two or more, mutually constructing understanding, solutions, meanings, applications, or products. Although there is wide variability in collaborative activities, most emphasize the learners' exploration and interpretation of the course material to an equal or greater extent than the teacher's explanation of it. Social needs and the challenge to create something together energize the group. Brainstorming is a classic example of an introductory way to use this strategy. (Cooperative and collaborative learning are described in greater depth by Will in Chapter Three.)

Some might say that if the group is highly motivated to begin with, inclusion activities are not necessary. My experience is that it is wise at the beginning of a new workshop, even if the group is very cohesive, to provide the opportunity to feel their mutual respect. I cannot remember a single occasion where this pursuit has not worked to our advantage, either in learning outcomes, transfer, or solidarity.

Developing Attitude. The pragmatism of most adults makes *personal relevance* a key ingredient in developing a positive attitude at the outset of a workshop. Participants are extremely sensitive to the degree to which they can identify their perspectives, needs, and values in the content and processes of the workshop. Relevance occurs when learning reflects the personal, communal, and cultural meanings of the learners in a manner that shows a respectful awareness of their perspective. For example, two participants may both believe their company has to do something to diminish sexual harassment, the workshop's focus. However, what constitutes sexual harassment may be quite different for each participant. A relevant workshop will have to respectfully address both points of view.

Relevance leads to what human beings experience as interest, the emotional nutrient for a positive attitude toward learning. When we feel interested, we have to make choices to follow that interest in the most meaningful way. That is why *choice* can also be so important in developing a positive attitude toward learning. When we teach multicultural groups, we often do not know all the possible meanings, so choices of specifically what to learn (topics and examples) and how to learn (learning styles and intelligences) may need to be determined by the participants. Using the topic of sexual harassment again, one learner may prefer to analyze court decisions while the other may prefer to role play a manager dealing with a complaint. Two strategies likely to have enough flexibility to develop a positive attitude in the beginning of a workshop follow.

Make the learning activity an irresistible invitation to learn. The first time people experience anything that is new or occurs in a different setting, they are forming an impression that will have a lasting impact. Making the first learning experience in a workshop an irresistible invitation to learn is essential. The way to achieve such an effect is to garner the intrinsic motivation that occurs when the following five criteria are met by the learning activity itself.

1. Safe: There is little risk of the participants suffering any form of personal embarrassment from lack of knowledge, personal self-disclosure, or a hostile or arrogant social environment.
2. Successful: There is some form of acknowledgment, consequence, or product that shows that the participants are effective or, at the very least, that their effort is worthwhile.
3. Interesting: The learning activity has some parts that are engaging, challenging, or at least stimulating.

4. Self-determined: Participants are encouraged to make choices about their behavior (for example, what they share, how they learn, what they learn, when they learn, with whom they learn, or how they are assessed) based on their values, needs, concerns, or feelings. At the very least, participants have an opportunity to voice their perspectives.

5. Personally relevant: Prior participant experiences, concerns, or interests are used to create elements of the learning activity, or the teacher develops the experience in concert with the learners.

The author experienced an example of this strategy in a workshop on adapting to the culture of another country. The initial learning activity focused on learning important expressions in the language of that country. The instructor began by asking the participants which expressions they most wanted to learn and recorded them on a flip chart: "hello, goodbye, where is the bathroom? how much does this cost?" With this method, she met the criteria of *personally relevant* and *self-determined*. After she taught us the expressions, she asked us to pick a partner and practice until we felt proficient. We could then move on to another partner for further practice. *Safety* was maintained by keeping the group small (a dyad). *Success* was immediate, and it was *interesting* to practice with two different people. It was also fun, and participants from that moment forward used these expressions during breaks and free time.

Use relevant learning models. Any time participants can witness people similar to themselves (in age, gender, ethnicity, class, and so on) competently performing the desired learning goal, their self-confidence is heightened; they are prone to believe that they too possess the capabilities to master comparable activities. People with whom participants can identify also convey information more likely to be relevant to the perspectives and values of the participants themselves. With film and video technology we have creative and economical ways to offer learners vicarious examples that are pertinent and realistic. Past participants are an excellent source for live modeling sessions. For example, the teacher of a workshop on research methods could present a panel of past participants who have successfully conducted research to share their experiences and findings with current participants.

Enhancing Meaning. Meaning is created by workshop participants as they *engage* themselves in *challenging* learning activities. In *engagement* the learners are active and might be searching, evaluating, constructing, creating, or organizing some kind of learning material into new or better ideas, memories, skills, values, feelings, understandings, solutions, or decisions. Often there is a product created or a goal reached. Engagement is the process, and *challenge* is the opportunity. The challenge often has a goal-like quality and requires some degree of capacity, skill, or knowledge on the part of the learners, as in the case of solving a problem. A challenging learning experience in an engaging format about a relevant topic is intrinsically motivating because it increases the complexity of skill and knowledge about something important to the participants. Two challenging and engaging formats follow.

Posing a Problem. A problem is any situation in which a learner wants to achieve a goal for which an obstacle exists. This may be a condition of life, such as how to make higher education more available to low-income students. Or it may be more specific, such as how to solve a discipline problem at work. It can also be an academic problem taken from the field being studied, such as solving an accounting problem in a workshop on accounting. The more mystery, fascination, or intrigue the problem can pose, the better the learning experience will be.

Creating a Simulation. Simulations are learning procedures that include role playing, exercises, and games that allow participants to practice and apply their learning in ungenuine yet sufficiently realistic contexts. When participants can sincerely experience perspectives, ideas, skills, and situations approximating authentic instances of life, they have a real opportunity to enhance the meaning of what they are learning and to become more proficient. These methods are also excellent for the development of empathy and validation. They give learners the chance to take on the viewpoints and rationales of people from different backgrounds, as in the case of a lesbian couple and a heterosexual couple discussing the merits of a proposed law concerning domestic partnerships.

Engendering Competence. Competence is evidence that one is effective at what one values, and for adults, it is the raison d'être for workshops. It also is critical for transfer. Engendering competence usually occurs through some form of assessment that is *authentic* to the participants' world and that allows them to realize some degree of *effectiveness* with their new learning. Authentic assessment is connected to the learners' life circumstances, frames of reference, and values. For example, if a case study were used as an authentic assessment, it would require participants to respond to a situation that mirrors their work life with the resources and conditions that are normally available. Effectiveness is the learners' awareness of how well they know or can apply what they've learned. In the example of the case study, the learners would likely want feedback about how well their responses resolve the issues found in this case study to understand the effectiveness of those responses. Two strategies to develop participant confidence in realizing what they have learned follow.

Performance assessment is an evaluation task that reflects the breadth, depth, and development of participant learning; learning experiences connected to real-life needs of participants; and participant reflection and self-monitoring. Here is where the learning objectives for the workshop have extreme importance because they usually determine to a large extent the construction of this assessment. So if we said that as a result of the workshop, participants would be able *to describe three possible solutions to environmental problems in their industrial setting,* then at some time toward the end of the workshop we must give the participants a chance to do so. This may occur in response to a problem, a current event, a research description, or a video news analysis. Also, we will need some criteria for participants to judge their own effectiveness. These criteria could be predetermined or established by mutual consensus, expert judgment, or comparison to real-world examples. In fact, the more that participants are aware of effectively learning something, the more likely they will use what they have learned.

Feedback is information that learners receive about the quality of their work. Teacher comments about emerging skills and written notes on an assignment are forms of feedback. Feedback enhances participants' motivation because they are better able to evaluate their progress, locate their performance within a framework of understanding, correct their errors efficiently, and maintain their efforts toward realistic goals. In general, feedback is probably the most powerful process that teachers can regularly use to affect learners' competence. To elicit intrinsic motivation, feedback should be informational rather than controlling. It should emphasize the learners' increasing effectiveness rather than the teacher's personal approval. For example, "Your writing is well organized and concise. I appreciate the clarity of your work" rather than, "That's fine. You're meeting the standards *I've set* for business writing in this workshop."

Here are some further suggestions for feedback. Make feedback specific and constructive. Most people prefer specific information and realistic suggestions for how to improve. Make feedback prompt. Give it as quickly as the situation reasonably allows. Make feedback positive. Place emphasis on improvements and progress rather than deficiencies and mistakes.

Putting It All Together

One of the primary values of the Motivational Framework for Culturally Responsive Teaching is that it can be used as an organizational aid for designing workshops. As discussed in the previous sections, by continually attending to its four related conditions and questions, the teacher can select motivational strategies to apply throughout the entire workshop. The teacher translates these strategies into a set of sequenced learning activities that continuously evoke participant motivation and learning.

Table 2.1 is an example of a fully designed workshop with learning activities aligned with the motivational strategies that led to their creation. The workshop leader is a faculty development specialist conducting a workshop on the management of strong emotions during classroom controversy. The workshop is designed for fifteen faculty members, with a length of seven hours. Given the demographics of the campus, about 30 percent of the participants will be people of color, 40 percent will be women, and the age range is likely be thirty to sixty. The learning objective is: Faculty will identify and practice teaching and communication methods that can support learner emotions in a manner that allows for individual expression as well as continuing mutual respect.

The Motivational Framework for Culturally Responsive Teaching allows as many strategies as the teacher believes are needed. The teacher's knowledge of the participants' motivation and culture, workshop content, and time

Table 2.1. Workshop Plan Designed with the Use of the Motivational Framework for Culturally Responsive Teaching

Motivational Condition and Question	Motivational Strategy	Learning Activity
Establishing inclusion: How do I create or affirm a learning atmosphere in which participants feel respected and connected? (Beginning)	Multidimensional sharing	After participants have introduced themselves, they form small groups and share a topic or skill that they value teaching and that elicits strong emotions in them because of their cultural or social background.
	Collaborative learning	Participants brainstorm particular strident words, actions, triggers, or incidents that they find very challenging to manage. Teacher lists these on a flip chart.
Developing attitude: How do I create or affirm a favorable disposition toward learning through personal relevance and choice? (Beginning)	Make the learning activity an irresistible invitation to learn	Participants form triads and one (or more) of them shares a method he or she has used effectively to respond to one of the challenges listed. Groups report, and the teacher lists these methods next to the indicated challenges. Teacher circles those he or she will teach today and invites faculty to continue to share their insights and experience.
Enhancing meaning: How do I create engaging and challenging learning experiences that include learner perspectives and values? (Throughout)	Use a variety of presentation styles to convey four different concepts	Teacher uses an overhead projector and handouts to describe ground rules; uses an exercise to communicate the concept of "think, pair, share"; shows a short controversial video to which participants react by journaling; and uses volunteer models as a cooperative learning base group in action.
	Posing a problem	The teacher asks the participants to think of the language and attitudes of their students and to revise or add to the gound rules to make them more understandable and culturally respectful.

Table 2.1. Workshop Plan Designed with the Use of the Motivational Framework for Culturally Responsive Teaching (*Continued*)

Motivational Condition and Question	Motivational Strategy	Learning Activity
	Creating a simulation	Participants role-play a cooperative learning group discussing a controversial court decision involving gender issues.
Engendering competence: How do I create or affirm an understanding that participants have effectively learned something that they value and perceive as authentic to their real world? (Ending)	Performance assessment	Particpants respond to a case study in which a faculty member loses control of a class. Participants conceptualize what might have been done in the moment as well as what might have been done to prevent this incident.
	Feedback	Participants compare their responses to the case study with the suggestions of three faculty members who are experienced multicultural educators.
	Feedback	Workshop concludes with each participant posting an action plan for his or her own course based on today's learning. The workshop leader and the participants visit the posters in carousel fashion to offer supportive comments and suggestions.

constraints will determine the quality and quantity of motivational strategies to use. This framework provides a holistic workshop design that includes a time orientation, a cultural perspective, and a logical method to elicit intrinsic motivation among adults from the beginning to the end of the workshop.

Based on field studies, a practical way to design workshops is to use the four motivational questions to select or create those motivational strategies that seem most likely to fulfill the four motivational conditions and then to reflect on each strategy to create an activity or process that will carry out the essence of the strategy.

Because design is a creative process and an act of composing, ideas for activities sometimes emerge prior to strategy selection. In this manner, strategies can be a suitable afterthought. In Table 2.1 almost all the strategies are selected from those presented in this chapter. For more possible strategies directly related to culturally responsive teaching see *Diversity and Motivation* (Wlodkowski and Ginsberg, 1995) and *Teaching for Diversity and Social Justice* (Bell, Adams, and Griffin, 1997).

The workshop in Table 2.1 ends with an action plan, an excellent device to increase the probability of transfer of new learning to the workplace. Action plans work like goal-setting strategies. They help participants organize what they are learning and clarify how to apply it to their real-world situations.

Concluding Comments

The learning acquired at workshops alters our lives. After reading, workshops are probably the primary educational experience by which we maintain our professional learning. Workshops are also the lifeblood for organizational improvement. They have the potential to be a concrete means for greater equity. Designing workshops with the Motivational Framework for Culturally Responsive Teaching is a way *to create learning experiences where inquiry, respect, and the opportunity for full participation by diverse people is the norm.* Whatever the pedagogical format, this is a goal worth accomplishing and an educational condition essential to learning in a free society.

References

Bell, L. A., Adams, M., and Griffin, P. *Teaching for Diversity and Social Justice: A Sourcebook.* New York: Routledge, 1997.

Csikszentmihalyi, M., and Csikszentmihalyi, I. S. *Optimal Experience: Psychological Studies of Flow in Consciousness.* New York: Cambridge University Press, 1988.

Deci, E. L., and Ryan, R. M. *Intrinsic Motivation and Self-Determination in Human Behavior.* New York: Plenum, 1985.

Deci, E. L., and Ryan, R. M. "A Motivational Approach to Self: Integration in Personality." In R. Dienstbier (ed.), *Nebraska Symposium on Motivation.* Lincoln: University of Nebraska Press, 1991.

Kitayama, S., and Markus, H. R. (eds.). *Emotion and Culture: Empirical Studies of Mutual Influence.* Washington, D.C.: American Psychological Association, 1994.

Sue, D. W., and Sue, D. *Counseling the Culturally Different: Theory and Practice.* (2nd ed.) New York: Wiley, 1990.

Wlodkowski, R. J. *Enhancing Adult Motivation to Learn: A Guide to Improving Instruction and Increasing Learner Achievement.* San Francisco: Jossey-Bass, 1985.

Wlodkowski, R. J., and Ginsberg, M. B. *Diversity and Motivation: Culturally Responsive Teaching.* San Francisco: Jossey-Bass, 1995.

RAYMOND J. WLODKOWSKI is a research professor for the School for Professional Studies at Regis University in Denver.

Guidelines for effective group learning are offered in this chapter, along with specific activities employing small groups in workshops.

Group Learning in Workshops

Anne M. Will

The advantages of learning in groups are well known and widely documented. A growing body of research suggests that people are more likely to remember what they learn in small groups. They are also more likely to generate creative solutions to complex problems. The literature speaks of the value of a learning process that actively engages the learner, builds community and consensus, and honors the diversity of voices within the classroom or workplace. More practical benefits include improved retention of new information and greater "buy-in" to the process when each is allowed to contribute (Imel, 1996; Johnson, Johnson, and Smith, 1991; Kadel and Keehner, 1994).

These advantages are well known to adult and continuing educators. The question before us here is: How can group learning be successfully employed in a workshop? Given the limitations of time and the demands of content common to many workshops, the facilitator may be tempted to adopt the traditional lecture-discussion format as the most efficient delivery. At least there will be no question that the required information has been covered. There is, however, no reason to assume that what has been "covered" in this way has been learned and will be recalled later on.

This chapter offers some general guidelines for those seeking to incorporate small-group activities into workshops and training. First, I differentiate between cooperative and collaborative learning groups and suggest the kinds of activities best suited for each. Common characteristics of effective group learning are described, and then some specific types of activities suggested. I also offer some remarks on the pitfalls of small-group work and suggest how these might be avoided.

Cooperative and Collaborative Learning

In popular usage the terms *cooperative* and *collaborative* are synonymous, and the terms are often used interchangeably by adult educators as well. Although there are common elements, most theorists distinguish between the two (Bruffee, 1995; Cranton, 1996). Both cooperative and collaborative learning are characterized by focused discussion and problem-solving activities conducted by small groups of learners. Both seek to move beyond simply the mastery of new information to higher levels of thinking through the application and evaluation of new concepts. Both are experiential and interactive.

There are, however, significant differences between the two experiences. Cooperative learning has been described as "a structured process that requires learners to work together on a task, share information, and encourage and support each other" (Cranton, 1996, p. 26). Cooperative learning groups are usually formed with a single and specific task to perform. The instructor defines the content and the task, the outcomes are fairly predictable, and the emphasis is often on the acquisition of new information. Because learning in a social context is often more memorable than solitary learning (Johnson, Johnson, and Smith, 1991), cooperative learning groups reinforce the learning of each member through discussion and peer review. The application of new safety regulations to a variety of situations is an example of cooperative learning. A workshop in which participants teach one another different stages of a new procedure is another.

Collaborative learning, defined by MacGregor (1990) as "shared inquiry," is more open-ended. In collaborative learning groups, "individuals work together to construct knowledge rather than to discover objective truths" (Cranton, 1996, p. 27). The teacher or facilitator collaborates with learners to shape the content and offer resources and expertise; the outcomes are less predictable. A long-range planning session where the facilitator helps a group define its goals is an example of collaborative learning. Support groups, writing groups, and reading clubs are other kinds of collaborative groups.

By definition, collaborative learning recognizes that knowledge is socially constructed and assumes the negotiation of different perspectives. This process can be time-consuming but, depending on the goal of the workshop, might be the best approach. For example, the board of directors for a women's shelter must decide whether to patch up the building they are currently renting or undertake a major fund-raising campaign to build a new shelter. A community college finds that it has outgrown its mission statement and must redefine the goals of the institution. A school board must cut 10 percent from its budget. Each of these problems could be solved by administrative fiat, but this action might alienate many of those directly affected by the decision. By including and respecting a range of perspectives, a collaborative process will generate broader support.

Characteristics of Effective Group Learning

Group learning is an open-ended process and can be unpredictable. An understanding of the dynamics of group learning will help facilitate a successful experience.

Group Size and Structure. The optimum size for a small group in most situations is four or five people—large enough to provide a variety of perspectives but still small enough to allow everyone to participate. For short, very specific tasks, groups of two or three may be preferable. Likewise, more complex tasks may require more participants. However, it becomes increasingly difficult to ensure the productive participation of each member in groups larger than six (Johnson, Johnson, and Smith, 1991).

Ideally, groups should be heterogeneous with respect to age, gender, race, background, and interests. A diverse group offers a range of concerns and perspectives. In the exchange of different points of view, the group gains a much richer understanding. Each individual is more likely to be challenged by and to learn from the unfamiliar. Also, this diversity more closely reflects the reality of the business world in which many of us operate.

While a heterogeneous grouping is preferable, it may not be easily accomplished in a short workshop. Most commonly, groups are formed on the spot, often from those seated together. People tend to sit with friends and co-workers and not with an eye to diversity. To mix them up, the facilitator can have participants draw different pieces of colored paper and then group them by color. Or the facilitator can cut up several laminated pictures related to the task of the workshop, have everyone draw a piece, and ask them to find the pieces that complete the picture. Each of these procedures takes time and may result in some initial confusion as people move about and reestablish themselves. However, such strategies do get the whole group moving and talking to one another in the first critical moments of the workshop. Of course, no random strategy will guarantee group diversity. If necessary, some groups may simply have to be broken up.

In certain situations, however, it may be preferable to create homogeneous groups. For example, in an organizational long-range planning session, the facilitator may choose to group people by department or division so that each unit can identify its needs and concerns. It would be wise to re-form the groups later in the session so that people from different divisions will have the occasion to share these concerns with one another. This "jigsaw" process is detailed below.

Group Process. Many adult learners are resistant to small-group learning. Busy professionals may resent the time required for group process. People who have had bad experiences with group learning may be reluctant to join in again. Typical complaints include uneven participation (the dominant member, the silent member), poorly defined tasks, no closure or follow-up (Swafford, 1995; Tiberius, 1989). Such problems can be minimized by careful attention to the process of group learning, allowing time for introductions, explanations, questions, and debriefing. At every stage, facilitators should provide clear guidelines and model appropriate behavior.

Warming Up. Thrown together with strangers, most people will maintain a polite reserve until they learn to trust and depend on one another. In the initial stages of group development, members of a group become acquainted and define the task at hand. It is therefore important to allow a few minutes for people to introduce themselves and begin to forge a group identity.

An ice-breaking activity will "thaw" the initial reticence of the group and begin to build trust among members. Start with some fairly safe but personal questions. Find out who in the group came the farthest to attend the workshop. Ask each person to disclose one unusual talent to the group. Each group could be asked to choose a title or a symbol based on the color or picture around which the group was formed. These apparently unrelated tasks are well worth the few minutes they require. When people are allowed to begin with relatively safe disclosures, they will be more comfortable sharing ideas and concerns later on. (Wlodkowski, in Chapter Two, also discusses the use of safe activities and exercises in designing inclusive and motivating workshops.)

Clarify Expectations and Ground Rules. Many groups fail for lack of clear guidelines and expectations. Both the goal for the exercise and the task to be performed should be explained at the outset. The goal is broadly stated: promoting industrial safety, learning new technologies, creating a new vision. This should be posted somewhere prominently. The task describes exactly what the group is expected to do and what each individual is to do within the group. If the task involves several steps, these should be written and distributed to each person. Describe how the exercise will end—with a presentation, a discussion, a simulation, or a test. How will the groups and individuals be accountable for their learning?

It is a mistake to assume that people know how to interact effectively in groups. It has often been noted that cooperation is not an innate human quality (Johnson, Johnson, and Smith, 1991). This is unfortunately as true of adults as it is of children. Many group activities fail because participants have not been adequately coached on the necessary skills. The facilitator should provide an overview of the behaviors supportive of group learning. Basic ground rules would include these: reserve judgment, listen and offer feedback to one another, be willing to take risks and venture new ideas, encourage all members to speak and to participate, and view conflicts—if they emerge—as opportunities for learning.

Effective Group Discussion. Merely urging everyone to participate will not ensure that a constructive discussion occurs. Group activities should be structured to encourage participation. For example, different tasks can be assigned to each member of the group. One person can be the recorder, who writes down the main points of discussion. Another can be the reporter, who reports back to the whole class what was decided by the group. A third person can be the gatekeeper, who notes whether the group is on task, how much time remains, and who has not yet contributed. Another way to encourage participation is to ask each member of the group to check in from time to time. Members could begin by stating what they hope to learn from this workshop or what they feel they have to offer to the discussion.

Effective group discussion may be derailed for a variety of reasons, loosely identified as either communication problems or social problems. Some typical communication problems are interruptions, digressions, the domination of discussion by one individual, and difficulty getting to the point. Some social problems may include personality conflicts, competition between members, the hostile participant or nonparticipant, the advocacy of one point of view to the exclusion of all others, and inappropriate humor or behavior (McCartney, 1997). Obviously, not all these behaviors can be addressed in a workshop. The facilitator should be alert to these potential problems and intervene if necessary, bearing in mind that a certain amount of tension is often productive.

Learning Styles. Adults do not all learn in the same way. A workshop will be more successful if activities are structured to address different learning styles. Some people need time to assimilate new information; others learn better through discussion. Those who learn best by doing will favor group activities such as simulations and role-playing. Not everyone is comfortable with the rough give-and-take of a group discussion. Building in some silent processing time will allow individuals to frame their learning (Heimlich, 1996). Participants could begin by writing down whatever concerns they have about the subject of the workshop. Allow enough time for everyone to think the question through. Then ask them to share one or two of their concerns. This also encourages everyone to contribute.

Wrapping Up. A group activity should conclude with a check-in by all members. Each participant may be asked to share with the group what he or she considers the most important points to emerge from their discussion. It is not necessary that the group achieve consensus. The recorder notes the points of agreement among the group and identifies whatever divergent concepts have emerged. All viewpoints are included and reported back to the class.

Hands-on activities such as a drills or case studies should be debriefed with the instructor and the whole group. Participants may share any insights or frustrations they have experienced. If a drill has not gone well or a response was clearly unsuitable, the instructor needs to address this and allow discussion of what might have gone wrong. Often the problem lies with the design of the activity. This should be acknowledged and remedied.

If the purpose of the activity was to generate new ideas or to build consensus, the facilitator should indicate how these ideas will be used. What kind of follow-up is planned? Who will take responsibility for carrying out the suggestions made? People need to feel that the work of the group is meaningful if they are to take such activities seriously in the future.

Specific Activities

Depending on the content of the workshop, any number of activity designs may be appropriate. A few structures are suggested here.

Jigsaw. This two-stage activity works well with a topic that involves several different steps or points of view. Participants form home groups and then move on to specialty groups. Having mastered the material or concerns of their specialty groups, they return to their home groups to share this information. Let us say that the topic of the workshop is a new model for family counseling, which consists of four distinct steps. Participants begin by forming home groups of four. After introductions, each person counts off, one through four, and the groups re-form by number. Those in group one will discuss the first step of the process, those in group two the second step, and so on. The work of these specialty groups should be clearly defined. Perhaps there might be a case study for them to consider. Everyone should take good notes of the discussion and be prepared to share these with the home group. If the specialty groups are too large to work productively (more than seven or eight), they can be further divided. After the specialty groups have completed their task, participants return to their home groups. Now each person is responsible for sharing one step of the process with the rest of his or her group.

The jigsaw method can also be used to explore different aspects of a topic. For example, to consider the impact of a new school discipline policy, specialty groups could be formed to represent the interests of parents, teachers, students, and administrators. Each specialty group could list the advantages and disadvantages of the policy from that one perspective. Back in the home groups, each point of view is represented, and the group must make a recommendation that is satisfactory to all parties.

Table-Top Exercises. In these cooperative exercises, learners are provided with resources and given a specific task or problem to solve. Often the task is the application of new information or procedures to a specific situation. For example, given a matrix of the physical properties of certain toxic chemicals, learning groups must use the resources at hand—tables, books, computer programs—to complete the matrix. The information is concrete and specific. The process of arriving at an answer is as important as the data itself. Working together, participants reinforce one another's learning (Vince Kelly, interview, February 1997).

Drill or Simulation. According to industrial trainer Vince Kelly at Prince William Sound Community College, a realistic, hands-on drill requires careful planning but can be a powerful learning experience. After reviewing procedures for dealing with hazardous materials, Kelly takes his classes outside where a barrel lies on its side in the parking lot. Participants have no idea what is in it or how much may have spilled. From certain clues—a label on the barrel, which leads to a chemical database—they must determine the correct procedure and act accordingly. The trainer may assign roles within each group, or for a more complex but realistic simulation, each group could be required to organize itself.

It is important to structure a simulation so that everyone has a role to play. If the groups are too large, some may stand aside with nothing to do. However, given significant responsibilities, most learners will rise to the occasion. Apart from the obvious advantages of hands-on learning, such simulations allow the more experienced workers to share vital knowledge with newcomers. Kelly warns, however, that the trainer should be prepared for unexpected results. A group may decide to tackle the problem or may conclude from the data that it is not safe to proceed (Vince Kelly, interview, February 1997).

Reverse Roles. If the group in attendance consists of people in several different roles or positions, it may be helpful to ask them to switch roles and experience the topic from another perspective. Say, for example, trainers are reviewing the procedures for switching power at an electrical co-op. Everyone in attendance is either a lineman or a dispatcher, and the two must work together to be sure the power is off. This is a life-and-death matter, admitting no mistakes. By reversing roles and running a simulation, each side experiences the critical nature of their work (Vince Kelly, interview, February 1997).

Concluding Comments

Although it can be challenging to incorporate small-group activities in a workshop, it is well worth the effort. Small groups promote learning, retention, and application by presenting new information in context. Participants find their own experiences and insights validated. In a changing workplace, where human resources are more profitably cultivated than replaced, there are compelling arguments for training that is interactive and experiential. Working in small groups, adult learners practice cooperation, active listening, and creative problem solving—all important behaviors in the workplace, community, and home.

Group learning decenters the classroom and shifts responsibility from the teacher or facilitator to the learner. Facilitators of small groups should be prepared to yield some authority. The discussion may not go as planned; the group may have other ideas. Although expert in certain areas, facilitators cannot fully appreciate the needs, pressures, and limitations under which learners may work. Skillful trainers must be flexible enough to adapt their material to the needs of the audience and to allow group dynamics to unfold.

References

Bruffee, K. A. "Sharing Our Toys: Cooperative Learning Versus Collaborative Learning," *Change,* 1995, 27 (1), 12.

Cranton, P. "Types of Group Learning." In S. Imel (ed.), *Learning in Groups: Exploring Fundamental Principles, New Uses, and Emerging Opportunities.* New Directions for Adult and Continuing Education, no. 71. San Francisco: Jossey-Bass, 1996.

Heimlich, J. E. "Constructing Group Learning." In S. Imel (ed.), *Learning in Groups: Exploring Fundamental Principles, New Uses, and Emerging Opportunities.* New Directions for Adult and Continuing Education, no. 71. San Francisco: Jossey-Bass, 1996.

Imel, S. (ed.). *Learning in Groups: Exploring Fundamental Principles, New Uses, and Emerging Opportunities.* New Directions for Adult and Continuing Education, no. 71. San Francisco: Jossey-Bass, 1996.

Johnson, D. W., Johnson, R. T., and Smith, K. A. *Cooperative Learning: Increasing College Faculty Instructional Productivity.* Washington, D.C.: ASHE-ERIC Higher Education Report No. 4, 1991.

Kadel, S., and Keehner, J. A. *Collaborative Learning: A Sourcebook for Higher Education.* Vol. 2. Washington, D.C.: National Center on Postsecondary Teaching, Learning and Assessment, 1994.

MacGregor, J. *Collaborative Learning: Shared Inquiry as a Process of Reform.* New Directions for Teaching and Learning, no. 42. San Francisco: Jossey-Bass, 1990.

McCartney, K. A. "Praxis in Seminaring: A Collaborative Approach to Increasing Student Effectiveness When Learning in Groups." Unpublished doctoral dissertation, Union Institute, 1997.

Swafford, J. "'I Wish All My Groups Were Like This One': Facilitating Peer Interaction During Group Work." *Journal of Reading,* 1995, *38* (8), 626–631.

Tiberius, R. G. *Small Group Teaching: A Trouble-Shooting Guide.* Ontario Institute for Studies in Education, Monograph Series, no. 22. Ontario: OISE Press, 1989.

ANNE M. WILL is an associate professor of history and social science at Prince William Sound Community College in Valdez, Alaska.

Workshops could be more effective for all learners if planners and teachers paid more attention to power dynamics.

Negotiating Power Dynamics in Workshops

Juanita Johnson-Bailey, Ronald M. Cervero

Workshops are conducted in social and organizational settings in which social power is distributed along many dimensions. It is important to recognize that teachers' and learners' positions and therefore power in these social and organizational hierarchies fundamentally affect what is taught and learned in workshops. Our basic viewpoint is that although power relationships provide the grounds on which all teaching and learning occur, their effect on workshops has rarely been addressed. The problem, therefore, is that workshops are not as effective as they could be because planners and teachers have not paid systematic attention to these issues. Our view asks you to see teachers and learners not as generic individuals but rather as people who have differential capacities to act (our definition of power) based on their place in the hierarchies of our social world.

In the first section of this chapter, we discuss the unique characteristics of workshops and explain why planners and teachers should expect the power relationships in the wider social and organizational contexts also to be a dynamic in the workshop setting. In the second section, we use material from the literature, from our own practices, and from the practices of associates and colleagues to illustrate how power dynamics can affect teaching and learning in workshops. The final section offers strategies for teaching effective workshops in the face of power relationships. We argue that once planners recognize the dynamics that are likely to play out in the workshop, they need to take action to both strengthen those that can nurture effective learning and counteract those that will inhibit such learning.

Are Workshops the Real World?

Nearly all discussions of the workshop in adult education simply avoid this question (Knowles, 1980). There seems to be an assumption that workshops happen in a universe parallel to the real world because the power relationships omnipresent in the social and organizational settings of everyday life are ignored. By stripping learners and teachers of their place in the hierarchies of social life, it appears we stage workshops where the politics of everyday life do not operate or matter. Workshop instructors and learners are seen as generic entities, unencumbered by the social structures that prescribe our social relationships. In a workshop one of us recently taught, the learners included several directors of training departments and their staffs. This fact offered many possibilities and constraints for teaching the workshop and for the transfer of learning afterward. By not recognizing the power dynamics that framed the relationships among these learners, opportunities for effective teaching would have been lost.

Another perspective also views workshops as not exactly the real world and moreover contends that this is precisely what contributes to their effectiveness. In the original sourcebook on workshops, Sork (1984, p. 7) argues that "the workshop participant is both an emigrant and an immigrant: He or she temporarily leaves one environment or social system and temporarily enters another. Although a certain amount of environmental baggage always accompanies learners to workshops, removing them from their natural setting for the time of the program isolates them from distractions and day-to-day concerns and enables them to concentrate on the problem at hand." In contrast to Knowles, this view acknowledges the learners' environmental baggage and further recognizes that this baggage can not be shed when participants attend a workshop. Thus, we could not have expected the supervisors of the training departments and their staffs to have shed those social roles for the three hours of instruction. Nevertheless, this baggage is still not seen as a source of insights for teaching. The emphasis continues to be placed on ignoring the baggage and focusing on creating a new environment in which these factors will not get in the way of effective learning. This view does ask us to see that teachers and learners are not generic individuals (we all have environmental baggage) but still requests that we treat people as if they were the same.

Our view, on the other hand, is that workshops are the real world because the power relationships that structure our social lives cannot possibly be checked at the door to the workshop setting. There is no magical transformation that occurs as teachers and learners step across the threshold of the classroom (Tisdell, 1995). McIntosh (1989) also uses the baggage metaphor by discussing white privilege and male privilege as important socially structured power relationships that affect our lives. These privileges are seen as an "*invisible weightless knapsack* [italics added] of special provisions, assurances, tools, maps, guides, codebooks, passports, visas, clothes, compass, emergency gear, and blank checks" that can be used in any situation. McIntosh, a white woman, provides honest examples, several of which are relevant to educational settings: I can be fairly sure of having my voice heard in a group in which I am the only member of my race; I am never asked to speak for all the people of my racial group; if I have low credibility as a leader, I can be sure that my race is not the problem; and I can speak in public to a powerful male group without putting my race on trial. McIntosh's analysis can be extended to include other ways that power shapes our social relations by understanding that the term *race* can be substituted with the terms that categorize members of other disenfranchised groups, such as gender, class, age, ability or disability, and sexual orientation. In this chapter we argue that workshops could be more effective for all learners if planners would accept this view and act on it.

Power Dynamics in Workshops. Given the characteristics of the workshop format, an understanding of power dynamics is particularly crucial. As Fleming states in the Editor's Notes: "The purpose of a workshop is to develop the individual competence of participants within a specific, well-defined area of need; emphasis is usually placed on the transfer and application of new learning. More specifically, a workshop provides for hands-on practice, thus giving it the character of a laboratory. A workshop is designed to be highly interactive and to support participants learning from one another; it is never an 'information dump.'" The characteristics outlined by Fleming do not suggest a one-way transfer of information in which power relations are generally nonnegotiable but rather that instructors and learners are involved in highly interactive relationships that need to be successfully negotiated. As Pankowski (1984, p. 22) concluded, "perhaps the most critical item on which the resource person can work is the structuring of the interactions among participants and between participants and resource people so that the time in the workshop can be both enjoyable and productive." She points out that good resource people make sure every learner has an equal opportunity to be heard and is protected from personal attack. She reviews a number of factors that have been shown to both inhibit and facilitate group interaction, including group size, group composition, the communication network within the group, group cohesiveness, and group leadership. Fox (1984) has focused on how power relationships in the learners' environments are potential obstacles to the transfer of new learning. He argues for workshop planners and teachers to attend to the "formal and informal rules of conduct, power and authority hierarchies, and formal and informal sanctions and rewards for performance" (p. 32) in the learners' work settings. Our perspective in this chapter is that the power relationships between learners and the instructor are important sets of conditional factors that affect the quality of the experience. As already suggested, the existing literature speaks universally of learners and their teachers as if their ages, personalities, cultural memberships, and abilities come together to make them individual carbon copies that occupy the workshop environment. However, our experiences as participants and workshop leaders tell us differently.

Disabling Myths: The Generic Teacher and Adult Learner

One formula does not fit all. Trainers can conduct the same workshop several times to what they believe are similar audiences yet encounter various reactions. What accounts for great or poor receptions? Participants can sit side by side in the same workshop and come away with different learning experiences and dissimilar impressions of the success or failure of the training. What accounts for these disparate accounts of the same incident? There can be many answers to both questions: the presentation of the workshop information, the time of day, the workshop setting, or the company culture. Variations among the learners based on different expectations, knowledge base, or background are other possible explanations. Perhaps the reason overlooked most often is the most obvious. Instructors and learners have different experiences in workshops because variances cannot be avoided. They should be expected because there are no generic instructors or learners (Johnson-Bailey, 1994).

Before discussing how the myths of the generic learner and workshop leader are manifested in our practices, we must first address positionality: who an instructor is as a person and who participants are as people. This factor influences the learning environment more than any other factor (hooks, 1994; Maher and Tetreault, 1994). Positionality is a multidimensional concept. One's positionality is determined by one's membership in major cultural groups. Gender, ethnicity, race, ability or disability, sexual orientation, age, and class are the significant identifiers of one's positionality, although many other individual and group considerations can influence one's personal outlook on life or political affiliations.

Since workshops occur in the real world, it follows that their participants bring real-world attitudes and opinions into the milieu. These perspectives were formed in our society, which is hierarchical, and they establish a linear ranking based on preferences. The way in which these frameworks operate in the workshop are twofold. First, workshop leaders and participants bring preset assumptions and beliefs regarding each other into the environment and second, they continue to act in predetermined and familiar ways toward one another. Quite often the ways in which people interact are habitual and unconscious. They have been formed by the ways in which we were socialized into our families and into the broader communities to which we belong.

For the purposes of this discussion we will concentrate on gender and race. This decision is based on several factors. First, we find that in our conversations with instructors, these issues are raised consistently more than others. We also see these systems of oppressions as wide-ranging and overarching. Finally, we feel that many of the dilemmas and recommendations relative to gender and race are applicable to the other concerns and that readers can easily transfer the knowledge.

The Gendered Dynamic. In our everyday world, men are commonly accepted in positions of leadership. This is evident in every facet of our society. Men compose the majority of our national and local leaders. This accepted and assumed power transfers to the workshop setting. So what happens when a workshop leader is a woman?

The answer is that gender affects the outcome. In our conversations with several women workshop leaders, stories of how gender affected the workshop were commonplace. One woman, who conducted a five-hour workshop for adult literacy trainers, recalled being constantly interrupted by a male participant who would give examples or ask questions. She eventually asked him to hold his questions until later, but he did not. She noted that his behavior had been different, even deferential, when he was a participant in a workshop run by her male colleague. His behavior followed a documented cultural norm in our society: men frequently interrupt women speakers (Sadker and Sadker, 1994).

Speaking and being listened to in our society is a privilege that is taken for granted by males in our culture. Being taught to speak less often and to seldom break into conversations is a behavior that is learned by females (Sadker and Sadker, 1994). This socialized issue of voice and silence affects the workshop environment in myriad ways. As participants, women often preface questions and statements with "This might not be important, but . . ." or "This may be a stupid question, but . . ." Even more unfortunate is when female participants do not speak at all. As workshop leaders, women unconsciously defer to male participants or, at the very least, endeavor not to violate a cultural norm by actively and publicly silencing a male speaker. The same behavior is replicated by male instructors who interrupt female speakers and who listen to and defer to male participants. The intent is seldom to actively advantage one group or person over another, but the outcome is to continue to follow our familiar routines.

Additional ways in which the phenomenon of gender alters the workshop setting have been noted. The behaviors displayed by participants during introductions and in small group activities are two areas where patterns of demeanor based on gender are commonly observed. The workshop leaders interviewed reported that most often in mixed groups when introductions are voluntary, the men routinely introduce themselves first or, on those occasions when they defer to women participants, make announcements such as, "Ladies first." This behavior could be based on the concept of women as the "other" and not women as "equal." In addition, it has been noted that the same pattern of deportment follows when volunteers are needed for activities. Men generally volunteer first and are thought to feel free to do so out of societal habituation. Further, when self-selection of seating occurs, women are noted to less often sit in positions of power, such as directly in front of the instructor or in aisle seats. While it is an unconscious behavior and not an exact science, where a person sits can convey how he or she will be viewed by fellow participants and by the workshop leader.

Gender can also determine how a workshop leader will be seen. It is not uncommon for women instructors to be criticized for not being sufficiently knowledgeable of the subject area, for being indecisive, and for being too flexible. Such assessments have been conveyed with the evaluative commentary: "I asked her a question and she did not know the answer," or "She gave us too many choices."

Such assessments of workshop leaders are discretionary and are based on how the participant views the leader. Positionality and the encompassing stereotypical light in which the instructor is seen emerge as important determinants of the effectiveness of the learning and teaching transaction. Saying you do not know an answer and giving a participant choices can be viewed positively just as easily as negatively. A speaker who enjoys conducting the workshop and is excited about the subject and an instructor who speaks so that everyone in the room can hear her are usually thought of as good traits in a workshop leader. However, the perspective of the viewer regulates how the action will be judged. Does the participant feel that a woman should be in this position of leadership? If not, then a woman's voice could be an irritant or a woman's enthusiastic leadership style could be seen as unacceptably offensive. The dissatisfied participant can use an unfair societal stereotype to evaluate the leader's performance, be they male or female, as either typical and therefore acceptable or as nontypical and therefore unacceptable.

The Racial and Ethnic Dynamic. Race and ethnicity also further affect the workshop climate and can be easily recognized by noting who takes part in training and who is most predictably absent from workshop leadership roles. There is no one group on which to focus. The region of the country will often circumscribe the racial or ethnic group most typically marginalized. Disenfranchised groups are viewed in opposition to their "normed" white counterparts. In Texas or New Mexico the disenfranchised group would be Mexican Americans, in South Dakota or Oklahoma it would be Native Americans, or in the southeastern United States, African Americans.

If the workshop leader is not a member of the majority group, a white American, issues of competency, credibility, and comfort can silence workshop inhabitants. A Mexican-American woman professor who also conducts workshops on human rights issues for her local city government confided that she was told that her accent was a noticeable communication barrier. As a native English speaker with a southern Texas accent, she could not understand the comment. Her only logical conclusion was that the learner had heard what she or he had wanted to hear and that her accent had been filtered through unaccepting ears.

Quite often workshop leaders who are members of disenfranchised groups receive paternalistic, but seemingly complimentary, evaluations such as "He was very articulate" or "She seemed very intelligent and well read." These statements speak glaringly about the participants' expectations concerning this minority group instructor. Would such statements be made about a white workshop leader? Why would a participant expect an instructor to be inarticulate and obtuse?

Learners and instructors alike in workshop settings continue to act on pre-conceived notions of each other. For example, issues of silence and voice are applicable when evaluating racial and gender power dynamics in workshops. Who speaks the most? Who seems most comfortable talking, interrupting, and moving around the environment? In many indirect ways participants both affirm and stifle each other. Their actions quite often could be based on how they operate in their daily lives. For instance, at the break during a five-hour workshop, an African-American workshop leader was approached by a white woman participant who related that she was afraid of a fellow participant, an African-American woman seated across from her. When asked to expand on her discomfort, she reported that the offending woman spoke forcefully and directly and did not couch her comments in niceties. The woman explained succinctly, "You black women just don't play that nice-nice game that we white women play." What is apparent in this example is that black women are seen as a monolithic group and the prevailing stereotype in this example portrays them as hostile. Again, the positionality of both actors in the scenario conspires to determine the interpretation. If a man or a white person spoke directly or forcefully, would he or she be viewed in a different light? It is not inconceivable that either would be perceived as charismatic and assertive.

Another example comes from an African-American instructor who reports always being asked in innocuous ways to present her credentials and to explain that she is not a token or "Affirmative Action" hire. For example, one male participant complimented her by first stating and then asking, "You're pretty sharp. You must not have come in on that Affirmative-Action bandwagon?" She confided later, "Well if I had, at that point I would have denied it. It was just a matter of not wanting to go down that road." Once more, the speaker, though his intentions were good, was operating from a lack of knowledge about the "other."

In talking with groups of workshop leaders, what became apparent was that women and members of disenfranchised groups face a dilemma not mentioned by any of the white male instructors. For example, they were occasionally faced with hostile, confrontational workshop participants who perceived that the leader had an agenda or perspective that viewed the majority or norm group negatively. These encounters happened regardless of whether the leader was offering a prepackaged program on a seemingly straightforward topic devoid of social implications or a workshop on cultural diversity. This seems to suggest that the problem is not contextual but rather specific to having a member from a nondominant group occupying a position of authority and disseminating knowledge. The instructors interviewed suggested this as the only possible explanation for these unexplained conflicts.

Beyond Facilitation in Workshops

It is evident that the dynamics that occur between participants and instructors in workshops are influenced by many factors. All human interactions, if studied, reveal ways in which power is ever present—sometimes balanced, sometimes unbalanced, but most often negotiated. The workshop is no different. Because this is an artificial and temporary learning setting, power dynamics are usually even more intense. In this section we discuss variables that affect interactions and then recommend ways in which an instructor can move beyond facilitation and attempt to successfully negotiate the power dynamics in the workshop setting. These recommendations are based on the literature, our own experiences, and the experiences of our colleagues.

Monitor the interactions in the workshop. Assure that learners will not unnecessarily interrupt each other. Pay particular attention to how learners who are members of powerful groups relate to participants of disenfranchised groups. Avoid the temptation to privilege in an attempt to correct this situation. If you use leaders in small groups, alternate between letting group members self-select and appointing group leaders yourself. Finally, know why your participants are there. Are they voluntary or involuntary? This is an important issue. According to Allard (1991), most are "prisoners, vacationers, and sponges." Using Allard's perspective, the *why* of participation can greatly affect how learners will behave. Since approximately 60 percent of a workshop is active participation (Kemerer, 1991) this recommendation is perhaps the most important to ensuring the health of the interaction. If the instructor does not actively watch the interactions in the workshop, the learning situation can be compromised.

Model appropriate behavior. Do not cross-talk when participants are talking. If someone else interrupts a participant, say, "Hold that thought, because I would really like to hear her or him out." Move around the room, alternating standing and sitting, and working with the participants when they are in small groups. Do not touch members, as touch can be an issue of power. People in power touch those who are in subordinate positions. It rarely works in reverse. Have participants move around so that no one person or group can control seats of power (next to the presenter) or form cliques.

Spend sufficient time at the beginning of the workshop assessing the backgrounds and abilities of participants. If possible, know who your participants are ahead of time. Find out about the cultures of the participants' workplace. For example, if the participants are all co-workers, you might be facing an intact group motivated either by loyalty or by a history of negative interactions. The entire atmosphere is also affected if both supervisors and employees attend the same workshop. The casualness of the workshop environment and the hierarchical management environment can collide.

Use visual materials that reflect different types of people, such as those of different genders, races, and abilities or disabilities. This provides an atmosphere of inclusiveness.

Use nonsexist and nonracist language. Remember that *he* is not a universal pronoun. Avoid referring to groups of people with descriptors such as *them*. Never include yourself in a group by using the term *we*.

Use wide-ranging examples that have diverse subjects as the actors. Note that most instructors and curriculum materials use examples that contain men and whites as the primary actors. Moreover, they are portrayed in positions of authority. Search for materials and use examples that do not reinforce stereotypes.

Vary the types of activities offered so that no one cultural pattern of communication is preferred more than another. For instance, activities that involve call-and-response activities, in which participants are asked to shout out answers, favor people who are used to actively and openly competing. Usually men and whites function better during such activities. Try to include activities that incorporate reflection and paired discourse. If you are going to use small groups, be aware that this is a prime activity to replicate patterns of interaction in existing societal hierarchies.

Perform consistent assessment to determine the power dynamics. We recommend a three-faceted approach. First, give participants three note cards at the beginning of the workshop. They can use these cards to ask or say anything anonymously that they do not feel comfortable saying aloud. Participants should deposit their first card in the box provided during the first break. Even if they have no comments or concerns, everyone should deposit a card so that anonymity is maintained. Second, at the midpoint of the workshop, ask them to perform the same task again. This time, however, the issues on the cards are discussed as part of the midworkshop evaluation. Finally, near the end of the workshop, give participants a brief, reflective break and encourage them to ask questions or make comments on their cards that will remain between the leader and the participant. Give them the choice of writing in a name and contact information.

Be constantly aware of the risk inherent in the workshop setting. Most participants and leaders will be unacquainted and expected to establish relationships in a short period of time. If you are drawn into a confrontation, make it a teachable moment by tying to connect it back to the workshop topic. Ask your learners to examine the confrontation and make it relevant to their workplace setting.

Remember that the environment will be affected by contextual and subject concerns. A training session that occurs at an employee's workplace will probably provide a less comfortable and nurturing surrounding than one that occurs in a neutral location. If an atmosphere that provides freedom of expression to participants is vital to success, discuss this dilemma with group members. It is also important for learners to know that what they can take back to their work setting depends on the willingness of the existing culture to accept change. There will be suggestions, recommendations, and knowledge gained during the workshop that will not transfer to their particular situations. Additionally, the subject of the training can greatly affect the experience. A workshop on cultural diversity or sexual harassment in the workplace will be wrought with political concerns and conflicting opinions. A training session on community volunteerism will be less controversial.

The applicability of these suggestions will vary in direct correlation to other factors, such as the length of the workshop (series or single event), subjects covered, and the individual style of the instructor. The setting could also be affected by participant grouping. Is the group an intact one in which the members have a prior relationship? Is there variation in the group based on job or educational levels?

Some of the ideas presented will be easily incorporated, whereas others will take practice. Some may not fit with your personal philosophy. However, it is hoped that the recommendations presented in this discussion will be viewed as guidelines for professional, ethically responsible practice that can be useful in managing power dynamics in the workshop setting. We are optimistic that the ideas and concepts covered will encourage you to see the workshop from a different perspective and to reassess the experiences you have had in that context either as an instructor or learner.

References

Allard, P. B. "Why They Didn't Learn What We Wanted Them to Learn." In T. J. Sork (ed.), *Mistakes Made and Lessons Learned: Overcoming Obstacles to Successful Program Planning.* New Directions for Adult and Continuing Education, no. 49. San Francisco: Jossey-Bass, 1991.

Fox, R. E. "Fostering Transfer of Learning to Work Environments." In T. J. Sork (ed.), *Designing and Implementing Effective Workshops.* New Directions for Adult and Continuing Education, no. 22. San Francisco: Jossey-Bass, 1984.

hooks, b. *Teaching to Transgress.* New York: Routledge, 1994.

Johnson-Bailey, J. *Making a Way out of No Way.* Doctoral dissertation, University of Georgia, 1994. *Dissertation Abstracts International,* 1994, *55,* 2681.

Kemerer, R. W. "Understanding the Application of Learning." In T. J. Sork (ed.), *Mistakes Made and Lessons Learned: Overcoming Obstacles to Successful Program Planning.* New Directions for Adult and Continuing Education, no 49. San Francisco: Jossey-Bass, 1991.

Knowles, M. *The Modern Practice of Adult Education.* New York: Cambridge Books, 1980.

Maher, F. A., and Tetreault, M. K. *The Feminist Classroom.* New York: Basic Books, 1994.

McIntosh, P. "White Privilege: Unpacking the Invisible Knapsack." *Peace and Freedom,* July/Aug. 1989, pp. 10–12.

Pankowski, M. L. "Creating Participatory, Task-Oriented Learning Environments." In T. J. Sork (ed.), *Designing and Implementing Effective Workshops.* New Directions for Adult and Continuing Education, no. 22. San Francisco: Jossey-Bass, 1984.

Sadker, M., and Sadker, D. *Failing at Fairness.* New York: Scribner, 1994.

Sork, T. J. "Designing and Implementing Effective Workshops." In T. J. Sork (ed.), *Mistakes Made and Lessons Learned: Overcoming Obstacles to Successful Program Planning.* New Directions for Adult and Continuing Education, no. 49. San Francisco: Jossey-Bass, 1991.

Tisdell, E. J. "Interlocking Systems of Power, Privilege, and Oppression in Adult Higher Education Classes." *Adult Education Quarterly,* 1995, *43* (4), 203–226.

JUANITA JOHNSON-BAILEY is an assistant professor in the Department of Adult Education and in the Women's Studies Program at the University of Georgia.

RONALD M. CERVERO is a professor in the Department of Adult Education at the University of Georgia.

Residential workshops provide a unique breadth and depth of learning experience for participants.

Residential Workshops

Gretchen Bersch, Jean Anderson Fleming

Anyone who has ever participated in residential education will tell you that it is a special experience. Although living and learning together is not for everyone, for many individuals it results in significant learning and change far different from that which happens in nonresidential programs. Residential workshops in particular can pack quite a punch over several weeks or even just a weekend. The purpose of this chapter is to examine the distinguishing characteristics of learning in residence, explore the participant experience, and discuss implications for the planning and delivery of residential workshops. By understanding the character and potential of this educational format, the decision to incorporate residence into workshops is simplified.

The Residential Experience

Knowles (1980) acknowledges that workshops are often residential, taking place "in hotels, resorts, or conference centers in which the participants live while attending the event" (p. 136). Residential workshops, as do all workshops, vary tremendously in length and design. In some, participants share living quarters; in others, they stay separately. In most, however, participants at least occupy a common facility, coming together for meals and for a common program of study. Perhaps the most generic definition depicts residential education simply as a format in which individuals live and learn together in the same place for the entire duration of their program. We can each draw from our own individual experiences in residential situations to add myriad details. The discussion here will be limited, however, to broader descriptions of this unique opportunity for learning: the possibilities created by residence, distinguishing features of residential programs, and the settings in which these programs frequently take place.

NEW DIRECTIONS FOR ADULT AND CONTINUING EDUCATION, no. 76, Winter 1997 © Jossey-Bass Publishers

Potential of Residential Education. The element of residence in educational programs provides the potential for creative program design and unique participant experience. Residence seems to offer sufficient time and comfort levels among participants for the incorporation of learning approaches that foster different ways of knowing for participants. Connected knowing, for example, as introduced by Belenky, Clinchy, Goldberger, and Tarule (1986), is easily recognized in descriptions of residential experiences: participants become more open to trying to understand another's point of view, they value personal experience as knowledge, and they are touched by and connected with their surroundings. There is a pervasive element of relationship in learning in residence, among individuals and between individuals and the subject of their study. In addition, the residential format helps individuals become immersed in their experience, quickening the pace and intensity with which interpersonal relationships develop and at which learning and individual change take place. Participants build relationships of depth and learn in ways different from the norm, and some change profoundly, even if only while within that world of the residential program.

We do not mean to assert, however, that individuals need residence in order to build relationships, learn, and change. We experience these phenomena all the time in our daily lives as well as in nonresidential programs. Residential education, however, seems to promote more rapid, yet more intense and more profound, changes than are probable with other formats. There remains just a hint of magic to learning in residence that defies certain description and that continues to set residential education apart. Houle (1971) notes that even N. F. S. Grundtvig, the originator of the residential Danish folk high schools begun in the mid-1800s, did not fully believe the mere process of living together could bring about some of the "maturity of viewpoint which arose from close communion between tutor and student. . . . Deeper, more profound ideas must be at work" (p. 6).

There thus appears to be no precise formula that will ensure this unique experience, although the usual elements do play a part: purpose and design of program, setting, participants, instructors, and so on. The combination of these elements, plus that touch of magic, can create a different atmosphere, one in which individuals are able to detach themselves from daily realities and relax in an uninterrupted continuum of experience. It is this detachment and continuity that Fleming (1996) maintains distinguishes residential learning and is largely responsible for facilitating participant immersion and creating intensity of experience.

Distinguishing Features of Residential Programs. The creation of detachment and continuity are among the first considerations in the planning and design of residential workshops. Detachment refers to both the physical and psychological isolation from the real world experienced by participants of residential education. It occurs as a result of both physical location and program design. Participants are separated and freed from pressures, roles, responsibilities, and routines of daily life; they are free to focus, concentrate, and reflect on themselves and their lives, in short, to immerse themselves in their experience.

Have you ever decided your work group should hold a longer-than-normal meeting because the purposes you hope to achieve just take more time and need a different feeling? You have decided it would be great to meet outside the workplace, and you schedule a two-day working retreat. Retreats make a nice change for participants, physically and psychologically detaching them from the workplace filled with daily pressures and interruptions. Your group will be out of the usual routine, away from the ringing telephones and demanding deadlines, and able to focus on the themes of the day. You schedule the retreat in a natural setting, one that is aesthetically appealing, where the pace of life is slower and the distracting temptations of cities are avoided. You also know it is important that participants be able to enjoy simple pleasures, taking walks outside to break up their days. You realize this type of retreat will help foster a renewed feeling of cohesion and will allow participants to be much more reflective, creative, focused, and productive. Simply stepping out of the fast lane and becoming detached from daily pressures creates vast potential for individual growth and change.

Detachment ensures continuity, and continuity enhances detachment. This second distinguishing feature, *continuity*, refers to the uninterrupted nature of residential learning programs. Individuals live and learn together on a continuous basis, twenty-four hours a day, for several days or weeks at a time. Continuity provides a greater number of opportunities than normal for informal personal interaction, for self-reflection, for critical discourse with colleagues, and for structured learning activity. Overall, there is a continuum of time in which to do, think, process, and reflect, to finish activities, thoughts, and discussions.

Two adult educators from Canada conduct a series of residential Mayors Institutes involving ten mayors from small towns in Canada and sometimes the northwestern United States. Each training session takes place in a remote but lovely wilderness setting for about five days. Having uninterrupted time free from distractions is a rarity for these leaders. This residential format provides a continuum that allows them time to think, reflect, and converse, to compare with each other the problems and solutions of their different but common situations. This same concept has been transferred to working with leaders in the Canadian national government, Africa, the Caribbean, and other locations around the world. In both the Mayors Institutes and the International Leaders Institutes, the residential format, physical setting, and program design mesh together to create the continuous detachment from the real world necessary for their success.

Setting. As previously indicated, residential workshops are frequently planned for remote, natural settings. Unusual settings in nature can provide a sense of adventure and authentic experience. For the past six years, Gretchen Bersch has invited noted adult education professors to teach in a residential setting on Yukon Island, in Kachemak Bay near Homer, Alaska. Although the primary stated purpose of these weekends is learning, building relationships and personal change characterize the participant experience as well. These weekends are perfect examples of the intensity of residential learning, of participants becoming immersed in their experience, and of the breadth and depth of learning and individual change that can occur.

Several years ago, Jerold Apps came to teach on Yukon Island. His vivid description communicates the power of settings to impress and imprint our experiences on us: "Snow capped mountains jut up from the opposite side of the bay, beautiful mountains with glaciers streaming down their sides. In the distance are a few commercial fishing boats; salmon season is open. And just around the corner from our meeting place, which is around a campfire on the beach, a pair of bald eagles is nesting. We see them often, soaring overhead. I mustn't forget the sea otters . . . and puffins for which this place is noted" [Apps, 1995, p. 11].

Yukon Island provides a multisensory experience that seems to heighten learning and magnify feelings. Just being in such a different setting may provide a disorienting dilemma for participants, which may be the first step in a process of personal or perspective transformation. In places such as Yukon Island that lack the usual routine amenities, people shift from being concerned with material comforts to focusing on their physical surroundings or the spiritual dimensions of their experience: there may be no running water nor electricity, but there is good food, great scenery, and great beauty. Perhaps there is indeed a healing power in nature that we can use to help learners relax and grow into their potential.

The Participant Experience

Fleming and Bersch, through research and personal experience, have both found that the participant experience in residential programs is characterized by three processes. Participants develop relationships with one another; they learn, often differently from their norm; and they undergo personal changes. It would seem workshop planners and leaders would want to capitalize on these built-in outcomes of residence.

To begin, participants of residential workshops come to know each other well, and quickly. On Yukon Island, for example, a quickened development of a sense of community, an intensity and depth of personal relationships, are present in each weekend. Year after year, both those who come to learn and the visiting professors have commented on this aspect in particular. Developing these bonds in such a short period of time would probably not be possible without a residential format. Program design that optimizes opportunities provided by residence reinforces the development of community as well, however. Evening sessions on the island with everyone gathered around the campfire set a climate of intimacy and closeness. The design and setting of the program can also add a facet of interdependence among participants, particularly if responsibilities for preparing meals or, in more remote settings, chopping wood for the fire, for example, are built into the daily routine. Although building interpersonal relationships may not be a stated workshop goal, it would take more energy to prevent it from happening than it does to allow, or even foster, its occurrence.

An added benefit of forming bonds with fellow participants is the facilitation of learning. Learning can become more vivid through group reinforcement and the mutual understandings deepened in the residential experience. Residence may act as a catalyst to enable, even enhance, learning, as participants have an increased amount of time for both formal and informal learning and for an increased diversity of learning opportunity. In other words, both quantity and quality of learning are potentially increased. The residential format allows for both planned and unanticipated, unstructured learning. Participants use their free time to think, talk, create, and explore new ways in which to learn and know. New learning also occurs serendipitously as learners are stretched beyond their personal limits and comfort zones. Often these challenges are the result of the constant interpersonal contact and the intimacy of that contact, both of which are physically imposed by residence.

Adult learning theory stresses the sharing of adult experience as a great resource for learning; the combined experience of adults is vast, varied, and vibrant. Apps (1995) again describes the weekends on Yukon Island, this time focusing on the learning that takes place:

> We meet, and think, and talk. . . . As we sit around the campfire . . . I introduce a few ideas, participants share their experiences. There is no pretension, no holding back, no reluctance to share personal stories. Stories from work, stories about organizations, stories about family, stories about challenge and opportunity. Stories about changing conditions. Stories about a changing Alaska . . . all are committed to Alaska . . . the wonderful location where we are meeting. I soon toss my agenda aside, my plan for what to do and when to do it. It is time to be flexible. To take advantage of where we are, and both learn the topic we are pursuing, and learn about the setting. . . . I offer some ideas. The participants offer perspective, context, application. We share, we exchange. Everyone is a teacher; everyone a learner. It's adult education at its best. (p. 11)

This description is not an atypical one for residential workshops. The learning, the knowledge created and shared by participants, bends and exceeds expectations. Original objectives are not lost, but they are overshadowed by even more significant learnings.

Finally, perhaps most varied are the descriptions participants give of the individual changes they attribute to residential programs. As might be expected, these changes are inextricably interwoven with learning. Being in such a different atmosphere seems to serve as a catalyst for individual change, for enhanced creativity, and for the emergence of new insights. The concept is not a new one, but residential education seems a quintessential example of its occurrence. Mezirow's (1991) model of transformative learning is also recognizable in participant descriptions of residential programs. Conditions are often ripe for the critical examination, either alone or with others, of the basic presuppositions underlying how we make sense of our experience and of the world around us.

Other changes experienced by participants are less profound, although they are no less significant for the individual. Seniors enrolled in residential Elderhostel programs, for example, have told Bersch that during their weeks as learners, they have felt more youthful and creative, and many have felt an expanded sense of self-awareness. Again, these comments are not uncommon among participants of residential programs. Rather than ignore this phenomenon of serendipitous change, planners and evaluators need to acknowledge and report it. Perhaps in this way, a more realistic picture of the potential of residential education can be painted.

Implications for Planners and Leaders of Residential Workshops

As indicated, residence and the opportunities created by residence can be powerful influences in any educational endeavor. A residential format, however, is a logistically complex undertaking and requires skilled facilitators to guide, orchestrate, and generally oversee the twenty-four-hour-a-day experience. In addition, residential education is usually expensive. With these concerns, the first consideration must be determining whether a residential format is necessary and desirable. Is it worth the effort? As with any educational format, its potential to support program goals must be evaluated. Can program goals be achieved with this format? Is this the best format I can select in which to achieve program goals? Is this format perhaps essential to achieving program goals?

The pros and cons of residence relate primarily to these two considerations: Will residence help me achieve and enhance my program goals? and Is a residential format logistically practical for me to undertake? The first question requires an examination of subject matter and of desired learning experience. For example, the content matter of many workshops quite frequently focuses on the development of job skills; this purpose may not require or benefit from the conditions created in residential formats. On the other hand, if team building or developing a graduate student cohort is the goal, a residential workshop may have the greatest potential for achieving this purpose, particularly within a limited amount of time. The detachment and continuity of residential formats can foster a quickened bonding among participants, which is central to the formation of teams and cohorts. Furthermore, the relationships developed in residence tend to last. For example, the sense of community developed among the participants of the Mayors Institutes mentioned earlier turned into a network of trusted colleagues to be called on once participants returned to their daily jobs.

In addition, formats can potentially ease, and even enhance, various approaches to teaching and learning. Some workshop leaders, for example, will be particularly interested in experiential or participatory learning, situated learning, and authentic activity. Often, residential workshops actually relieve some logistics attached to these instructional approaches. Residence allows participants to spend the maximum time possible in evocative settings or in settings similar to those where newly gained knowledge, skills, and insights will be applied. Other workshop leaders will be concerned with fostering perspective transformation or supporting connected knowing among participants. If personal change or exploration of attitudes, beliefs, work ethics, concepts of meaning, or knowledge is desired, residence may again provide optimal opportunities to create the conditions and relationships with which this examination may be initiated. Schacht (1960, p. 4) states that residential education "is especially adapted to the learning of attitude, understandings, concepts, and appreciations." He further asserts residential situations "best afford that opportunity for a re-evaluation of social, political, and personal philosophy which is not only at the bottom of citizenship but of all cultural life" (p. 4). Learning and change take place in residential education within a social context that effectively serves to multiply its potential impact on individual lives and communities.

The residential format, when matched with compatible program goals, therefore can help optimize the restricted time frames of workshops. By simply having participants on site twenty-four hours a day, residence provides the opportunity to incorporate a greater number and variety of learning activities than usual, as well as allowing time for reinforcement of learning through discussion and critical reflection. In addition, residence naturally highlights the physical setting of a workshop and its role as an effective tool in achieving learning outcomes.

The drawbacks most frequently associated with residence fall mainly into two categories: logistics and participant characteristics. Residential workshops, even more than other formats perhaps, require varied expertise, extensive logistical planning, and appropriate settings. It takes a great deal of skill to create conditions of detachment and continuity. Expertise in group process and in selecting and creating safe, conducive learning environments (physical, psychological, and sociocultural) is essential. At the most basic level, the availability or even the desire of people to be away from home for extended periods of time may negate the possibility of a residential program from the start. As stated at the beginning of this chapter, residential education is not for everyone. Some individuals do not do well in strange locations, living with strangers, and may not find learning in groups to be easy, desirable, or helpful.

Finally, as with any educational undertaking, unanticipated events will occur. This phenomenon is of particular significance for planners of residential workshops, however. Planners must expect the unexpected and plan for the unplanned. The unintended experiences are often particularly poignant features of residential learning. The planned, unstructured times become the times that help to differentiate residential experiences from nonresidential programs. Workshop planners can build in time for reflection, for conversation, for walks in nature, and, ironically, for serendipity. Planners and leaders, logically, should make the most of the opportunities provided by residence and of the atmosphere of continuous detachment of residence to go beyond goals of acquisition of knowledge and skills to include the examination of self and our relationship to others and to the world in which we live.

Concluding Comments

We have tried to communicate in this chapter the special character and potential power of residential workshops. The two distinguishing features of residential programs, detachment and continuity, help create the different atmosphere in which participants describe a breadth and depth of experience rarely found in nonresidential programs. Rapidity and intensity in building relationships, in learning, and in individual change further characterize the participant experience in residential education. Planners and leaders of residential workshops, while respecting the challenges presented by this format, should also recognize both the tangible opportunities presented by residence and the intangible magic of the residential experience.

References

Apps, J. E. "Teaching on Yukon Island." *Lifelong Learning Today,* 1995, 1 (3), 11.

Belenky, M. F., Clinchy, B. M., Goldberger, N. R., and Tarule, J. M. *Women's Ways of Knowing: The Development of Self, Voice, and Mind.* New York: Basic Books, 1986.

Fleming, J. E. A. *Participant Perceptions of Residential Learning.* Doctoral dissertation, University of Northern Colorado, 1996. *Dissertation Abstracts International,* 57–08, 97–01957.

Houle, C. O. *Residential Continuing Education.* Syracuse, N.Y.: Syracuse University Press, 1971.

Knowles, M. S. *The Modern Practice of Adult Education: From Pedagogy to Andragogy.* Englewood Cliffs, N.J.: Prentice Hall, 1980.

Mezirow, J. "Conclusion: Toward Transformative Learning and Emancipatory Education." In J. Mezirow and Associates (eds.), *Fostering Critical Reflection in Adulthood: A Guide to Transformative and Emancipatory Learning.* San Francisco: Jossey-Bass, 1991.

Schacht, R. H. *Weekend Learning in the United States.* Brookline, Mass.: Center for the Study of Liberal Education for Adults, 1960. (ED 030 828)

GRETCHEN BERSCH is a professor emeritus of the University of Alaska, Anchorage.

JEAN ANDERSON FLEMING is assistant professor of adult and community education at Ball State University, Muncie, Indiana.

When learners cannot come to our workshops, we can come to them!

Workshops at a Distance

Chere Campbell Gibson, Terry L. Gibson

And there it was—the workshop of your dreams! But on further reading, reality intervened. Just the cost of getting there was prohibitive even if you did stay over a Saturday night. Then, of course, there was the loss of weekend time with the family and lost time at work during the most critical time of the year. No, this was yet another workshop that would have to be missed.

Sadly enough the foregoing scenario is fairly typical. Perhaps you have been in a similar position. You have found a workshop that would be perfect in which to learn new skills or hone old ones, but the cost in dollars, energy, and time away from work and family just cannot be justified. Or perhaps you have been the workshop designer and have determined that it is important to offer your workshop multiple times around the country to regionalize the educational program and lessen travel costs for potential participants. You then discover resource people are reluctant to spend that much time traveling and being away from their family and work obligations. You just can't win! Or can you?

Let us look at some of the ways we can come to our learners and how we can design workshops using these new tools. Also, let us examine some of the unique considerations of distance delivery that move us from simply providing access to information to enabling the learner to have a successful learning experience.

Instructional Technologies and Continuing Education

One possible solution is the use of instructional technologies to provide workshops to learners who otherwise might not be able to join you and your resource people face to face. Education and training at a distance is not a new idea, but deciding how to reach potential workshop participants becomes the

NEW DIRECTIONS FOR ADULT AND CONTINUING EDUCATION, no. 76, Winter 1997 © Jossey-Bass Publishers

next dilemma. Our choices of potential instructional media are considerable and varied, and some even have a fairly lengthy history of use.

The technology with the longest history of use is, of course, print, with its one-hundred-plus years of service to education and training. Countless packaged programs have arrived at front doors around the world containing printed instructions and materials requiring assembly, experimentation, and the like. Community members can also serve as learning resources, providing a source of interaction, in addition to the instructor who is at some distance from the learner.

More recently, technologies that feature an interactive audio component have proven popular. One particularly effective and relatively inexpensive example is audioconferencing, with its almost forty-year history of use in continuing education. Resembling a large telephone party line (individual phone lines bridged together), learners gather at sites in small groups or as individuals at a convenient telephone to receive, discuss, and apply information of interest. The earliest use of this technology was continuing medical education. Through the use of audioconferencing, physicians have been able to remain in their home communities, rural or urban, yet enjoy access to timely information vital to their practice. For example, short presentations on the newest developments in medicine can be followed by case-based learning and small-group discussion. In this way, physicians, nurses, dietitians, and other health practitioners have been able to both access the specialized expertise of health care resources, and explore applications and implications of the latest breakthroughs in medical research with practitioners from around the country or the world.

The advent of audiographics has allowed us to combine the interactive capabilities of audioconferencing with the use of computer technology to transmit visual images to remote television monitors, thus supplementing audio-based instruction. Graphics, data, drawings, and images of objects can be conveyed through the use of a graphics tablet or a digitizing camera. Imagine teaching systems engineering where systems diagrams can be generated by small groups at sites around the world and presented for critique by their collective colleagues and co-learners. The interactive visual component of audiographics even allows annotations by remote groups while the interactive audio portion allows for both presentation and reaction by participants. The use of audiographics for the design of ad campaigns in business and other graphics design–related fields, such as landscape architecture, also come to mind.

Videoconferencing adds a motion component not available in audiographics. Through ISDN lines, the Internet, and satellite, cable, or microwave transmission, remote sites are able to see motion displayed on local screens. In instances where it is important to see procedures, as in medicine, or to view body movements, as in physical therapy or dance, videoconferencing provides a potential instructional solution. Be it one-way video from an origination site to many locations around the world or compressed, full-motion, two-way video, which most closely replicates the traditional face-to-face classroom, par-

ticipants are able to discuss what they see and, with two-way video, even replicate the actions for others to evaluate.

However, audio, audiographics, and video-based instruction occur in real
time, diminishing flexibility in time, place, and pace of learning. Costs and
video quality are also considerations. But uses have been diverse, ranging from
training in computer applications for support staff at remote sites, to presentations, interviews, and group problem solving regarding homelessness in the
United States.

We would be remiss if we did not consider computer conferencing, in
which learners and resource people interact via a computer network. Messages
in this largely text-based medium may be sent in real time (synchronous chats)
or delayed time (asynchronously), which allows for maximum flexibility in
reading and responding. In some ways, computer conferencing is reminiscent
of print-based instruction, but the ability to interact easily with multiple recip-
ients, live, adds an exciting dimension. Application of this technology includes
continuing professional education in veterinary medicine and adult education,
in which shared text documents are particularly conducive to facilitating collaborative learning and problem solving. World Wide Web technologies enable
us to add an interactive graphics component to our teaching and learning. CD-
ROM and multimedia can also supplement your remote workshop. And, in
the not too distant future, both audio and video transmission via the World
Wide Web will be perfected, providing us with yet another alternative for offering workshops at a distance.

Of course we must not forget that these instructional technologies can be
mixed and matched. Print is a usual component, regardless of technology. It
still remains very portable and, along with computer conferencing, provides
one of the best options for flexibility in time, place, and pace of learning. A
favorite example of the creative mix of technologies is "Raising Responsible
Teens," a program of the University of Wisconsin-Extension, which utilizes
satellite-based education to link child development experts with parents
around the country. Parents gather at community sites where local resource
people such as school psychologists and guidance counselors, law enforcement
personnel, and social service agency workers join them. Interspersed with
short lecturettes by national resource people, the local resource people work
with parents and often the teens themselves, providing consultation, participating in small-group work, and contributing to the discussion of local solutions to national problems. Later in the week, after parents and local experts
have been able to relate the material from the workshop to individual family
situations, audioconferencing is used to address individuals' questions posed
anonymously. Printed materials provide additional content resources for future
reference.

The key is that we consider the strengths and weaknesses of each instructional technology both in terms of our audience and what we hope to accomplish in our education and training. We can then select the winning combination
that will allow us to provide an engaging and interactive workshop.

Designing a Workshop for Distance Learners

A quick look at most adult education texts and articles on program-planning principles highlights the importance of assessing learners needs, defining learning objectives based on learner needs, identifying learning activities to meet these learning objectives, sequencing the established learning experiences, and evaluating the extent to which the desired outcomes have been achieved (Apps, 1979). Cervero and Wilson (1994, p. 3) suggest that "[t]he planning literature has repeated this structure for so long that the theorists see it as a sine qua non of good program planning." Likewise, a review of the instructional design literature in distance education would yield similar principles. So, for the most part, good program planning looks fairly similar, be it for face-to-face or distance teaching and learning.

Unique Design Considerations. Perhaps what is most critical, however, is the differences that do exist as we move from planning face-to-face workshops to planning those offered at a distance through the use of instructional technologies.

Learner Considerations. These considerations are expanded in the context of planning workshops at a distance. Not only must we assess learners' needs and the usual learner characteristics, including age, gender, ethnicity, disabilities, learning preferences, and the like, we must also determine the instructional technologies to which our learners have access and experience for the purpose of learning. This information on learners' access to and experience with instructional technology will be essential for media selection in later stages of workshop development.

Nature of Learning Activities. Defining general learning goals and objectives and identifying the learning activities necessary to accomplish these instructional goals are common and critical tasks in the design and implementation of a workshop, be it face to face or at a distance. As we define these events of instruction, we need to continue to ask, What does the learner need to see, hear, feel, and do to accomplish the learning goals of the workshop? And yes, there are times when participants must come to one place for a face-to-face workshop to accomplish these goals and objectives. For example, GE Medical Systems, a maker of such equipment as systems for magnetic resonance imaging and computerized tomography scans, offers the majority of its training workshops at a distance through the use of its educational satellite system, audioteleconferencing, computer-based training, and print. However, if an engineer needs training on a specific piece of equipment to accomplish the learning objectives and that piece of equipment is not available at his or her location, GE Medical will bring this employee to a face-to-face workshop at its headquarters in Wisconsin.

But GE Medical Systems also carefully considers the sequencing of learning activities. Often by providing appropriate training at a distance before the face-to-face portion of the workshop, the company can minimize the training time at corporate headquarters in Wisconsin, away from family and work. Further, with careful planning, additional follow-up training can be provided at a distance—a less costly and equally effective alternative according to GE's studies (Gibson and Gibson, 1995/96).

Media Selection. What comes next is particularly critical in the distance education context—the media selection process. After adding the data on learner needs, demographics, and access to instructional technology to workshop learning goals and objectives and sequenced educational activities, we must now determine which medium or media will enable us to accomplish the desired ends with maximal effectiveness and minimal cost. Monomedium thinking is of particular concern. No one medium is ideal. What is key is that the strengths of one medium offset the weaknesses of another through the use of multiple media. Media vary in their suitability for different educational tasks, and thus media selection must be "content-driven rather than technology-driven" (Dutton and Lievrouw, 1982, p. 113). We need to revisit the question, What does the learner need to see, hear, feel, and do to accomplish the learning goals of the workshop? Ideally, technologies are selected on their instructional merit, not their novelty nor political or other criteria. We need to consider the educational content, the need for interaction among and between participants, and the nature of the desired learning outcomes as a basis for our instructional technology choices. In addition, as already mentioned, we need to determine the characteristics of our learners in terms of access to and experience with learning via technology. Cost considerations cannot be overlooked either!

Sadly enough, research findings to date provide limited guidance on media selection. In metanalyses of media comparison studies focused on comparing achievement in a face-to-face environment versus the same instruction provided at a distance by any number and variety of media, the achievement of those instructed at a distance is equal to and often significantly greater than those taught face to face (Clark, 1983). The lack of guidance available to date combined with the documented potential of distance education strongly substantiates the need for further research. Continuing education practitioners need additional assistance in making better media selections—selections based on an understanding of the strengths of available media relative to the nature of the content, learning goals, events of instruction, and intended audience of the educational program.

Access Is Not Equal to Success

As we consider providing workshops through the use of instructional technology, we strive to provide a quality educational experience by remembering that it takes more than access to information to ensure successful learning. For example, imagine you are a financial planner in rural Alabama and are taking a workshop originating from Los Angeles, California. This workshop is presented via one-way video and two-way audioconferencing. You receive the educational program, that is, you can see and hear the presenter, but the instructor talks too fast and you do not understand what he is trying to teach. The print-based material is even less help, even though it did arrive in a timely manner and you did attempt to do the advanced reading and problem sets on estate planning. You have access to information, but you cannot learn it. You have no learning success. The technology has made it possible for you to receive new information, the access that we noted as so important, but many of the factors that have a major influence on the success of the educational experience are missing. These are the human factors. They fall under a general category of support and include technical support, instructor support, learner support, and administrative support.

Technical Support. Perhaps the most obvious kind of support that we think about in distance education is technical support. We quickly think about the help needed to ensure that we have the necessary system available. We need technical support to design the appropriate technical infrastructure, the phone bridges or the satellite downlinks positioned about the country, for example, and the interconnectivity of the technologies. In addition, it is important to have knowledgeable people to operate the equipment, such as printing press operators, camerapeople, audio technicians, and computer technologists. We also need people to maintain the technologies we use, keeping printing presses, audio or video bridges, cameras, editing equipment, and computer networks operating. And last, we need those who both have the technical expertise and are forward-looking to help us plan for the future of distance education by alerting us to changes in the fast moving world of technology.

Instructor Support. But what about instructors? Few continuing education instructors have ever learned at a distance; even fewer have ever taught a workshop at a distance using instructional technology. Instructors need support as well. They need help selecting the appropriate technologies. We often find that instructors like to teach with only the newest technology and learners feel they must learn with the latest technologies too. The newest technology is not always the best technology for the job, however, and usually it is not the most cost effective either. Who will help the instructors design their courses? Who will help them think about their learning objectives and how selecting the appropriate mix of technologies can help meet those objectives? Who will help them design for maximum learner-to-learner and learner-to-instructor interaction? Who will help these instructors learn to teach at a distance, to recognize that these new instructional technologies not only enable but also require us to teach in different ways? Who will help them consider the research on teaching and learning at a distance? Instructors, too, need lots of support.

Learner Support. Our learners need support as well. Research suggests that many learners are worried about learning at a distance (Gibson, 1996). For some, not having the instructor with them is a new way of learning. We need to help learners learn at a distance: how to manage time and stress, how to organize a place for learning, how to take responsibility for their learning. In addition, we need to help them learn how to learn with technology. Viewing an adult basic education lesson via satellite on a monitor is not the same as watching a popular movie or television show. New skills are needed to be an effective learner.

What about the learners and their need for technical support? If you are using print as a distance education technology and the book does not come in the mail, you need someone who will help resolve this problem. How can you learn if the books or CD-ROM does not arrive at your home or workplace? If the sound or picture is a problem in audio or video instruction, whom do you call if you are learning at home or in a small group at a work site? If learners cannot hear the lesson or see the demonstration, how can they learn? And what if learners cannot load the software? What if they cannot connect to the Internet to engage in problem-based learning with colleagues around the country? Again, whom do they call? Quality is hard to achieve, almost impossible, without technical support for our learners.

Further, what do your learners do to get answers to their questions about the content of the workshop? If the program is satellite based, is there someone on site to facilitate discussion and answer questions on small-group problem-solving tasks? Is there a facilitator for the audioconference? Are the computer conferences so vital to your discussions and applications of the content moderated? Learners need lots of support to ensure active and successful learning.

Administrative Support. Last but not least, it is also important to those of us who use distance education for providing continuing education to have administrators who have a vision. We need administrators who have an understanding of what the use of instructional technology can do, who have specific goals and objectives for their organization's involvement in distance education, and who understand what it will take to get there. We need administrators who ensure that the necessary technical systems are in place but who also make sure that the necessary human infrastructure of support for the instructors and the learners is in place. Administrators are needed who will ensure appropriate policies are in place. Often old policies get in the way of new distance education efforts and need to be changed to meet the demands of new paradigms of teaching and learning. And yes, fiscal support from these administrators is essential. As Glenn Farrell, a colleague in Canada who is the head of the Open Learning Agency, said, "The technology is dead easy. It's making sure the other parts and pieces are in place and working well, that is tricky" (Gibson and Gibson, 1995/96).

It does seem that a lot of support is needed. But think of that face-to-face workshop. Are we not constantly requiring technical support for the array of technologies our resource people bring to our programs? Do we not periodically provide orientation or overview sessions to our participants who might be new to a particular content area or field of practice? Have we not tried to help instructors consider new teaching and learning strategies to engage learners in a workshop? Support is indeed vital in both contexts.

Teaming for Success

But, you say, this distance education does seem like a lot of work. Although the actual workshop design process seems very familiar and adding instructional technology seems fairly straightforward, considering the array of necessary support, distance education still seems rather overwhelming. This is perhaps where adult educators, especially continuing educators, have an edge over the face-to-face instructor in the traditional classroom. The classroom instructor is used to working alone in planning, implementing, and evaluating his or her instruction. In contrast, the educator engaged in planning, implementing, and evaluating continuing education programs is used to working with an advisory committee comprising potential learners, subject matter specialists, audiovisual technicians, graphic artists, printers, marketing professionals, facilities and food service managers, and budget controllers. Designing and delivering an educational workshop has always been a team effort. Distance education just changes the team members to ensure that we have not only the necessary technical infrastructure to provide access to our workshops but also the necessary human infrastructure to support our instructors and learners to ensure a successful teaching and learning experience.

But Is It Worth All the Time and Effort?

This is a good question, and the answer depends on your criteria, the number and variety of which abound. Many educators will incorporate instructional technology into the design and delivery of continuing education to increase the numbers or diversity of participants. Others will measure workshop success on the basis of costs, while still others will strive for learning effectiveness.

Who Gets Left Out (and Who Gets Brought In)? One key consideration is who gets left out as we move to using instructional technology for the delivery of continuing education to lay and professional audiences. (Sork also addresses this question as he considers the ethical dimensions of workshop planning in Chapter One.) Our audiences have traditionally been white, middle class, urban, and well educated (Cross, 1981). As several experts note, "Successful managers need to prepare themselves to play a major part in addressing issues of equitable access to educational resources: equity in the composition of learners served by programming will be one of the fundamental questions raised about the proper use of telecommunications in education and training" (Dunning, Van Kekerix, and Zaborowski, 1993, p. 36). Technology based education allows us to overcome barriers of time, place, and pace and thus can provide access to instruction for those whose work and home responsibilities require flexibility in scheduling, for those in remote areas, and for those who are physically and mentally challenged. The use of instructional technologies that permit recording (video- or audio-based instruction), wide geographic distribution (audio-, video-, and computer-based conferencing), or individual pacing (print or computer conferencing) permit access to information where it otherwise might be impossible. But we must ensure access to the necessary technology, be it through libraries, educational institutions such as the Cooperative Extension Service or governmental agencies, or the wide array of human service agencies.

While research is limited, anecdotal reports and informal evaluations suggest a greater diversity in the ethnic background of participants in educational programs offered at a distance. But are our program materials culturally diverse in content, representing the wide range of ethnic groups, their language, literature, perspectives, cultural norms, and so on?

Further, a number of organizations have noted that in many instances up to 75 percent of the participants in these programs are new to the organization's programming. Are we ready for this increase in numbers of participants and the changes increased numbers require?

Will These Workshops Be More Cost Effective? A number of variables need to be considered in order to answer this question, including, for example, media selected, number of participants in the workshop, and the perceived value of reaching new audiences in remote areas. These costs need to be weighed against the costs (time, travel, multiple honoraria) of offering the workshop numerous times in multiple locations and the value of consistency of message. Experience in business, industry, and the military suggests that providing training workshops at a distance can be most cost effective (Chute, Balthazar, and Poston, 1989; Gibson and Gibson, 1995/96; Phelps, Wells, Ashworth, and Hahn, 1991).

But is it effective as we assess achievement? As noted earlier, comparisons of achievement of learners taught face to face versus at a distance using any one of a number of media have consistently demonstrated equal or greater achievement among learners at a distance. As Bates (1995) notes, every medium has its strengths and weaknesses in terms of its presentational qualities, the way it represents the world, its ability to handle concrete or abstract knowledge, and its ability to develop different types of skills (as distinct from presenting information). He suggests, "Technologies that combine strong presentational qualities with strong student control over the technology are particularly good for developing skills. Thus audio and videocassettes and multimedia are strong and radio and live televised lectures (unless taped for later replay) are poor for skills development" (Bates, 1995, p. 9).

Another consideration that cannot be overlooked is the element of workshop design. For example, some highly successful computer training has been conducted via satellite and one-way audio to Cooperative Extension offices throughout Wisconsin. It has been successful because of such design features as appropriate pacing for the learner; direct skills application at the work site during the program; and ample opportunity to raise questions, apply new skills, and solve problems with others during and after the training. A respondent in a recent study noted, "In my opinion most learning comes from application. . . . [S]itting there [you get] no skill acquisition" (Ottoson, 1997, p. 100). One advantage of conducting workshops in the participant's community or place of business is that the context for application is close at hand. A well-designed workshop using instructional technology will incorporate that context and the resource people within it. Often a six- to eight-hour workshop spans one or more weeks, with assigned tasks to be performed during the intervening period. The results are then shared with and critiqued by other workshop participants around the country. An example includes a multipart offering of workshops for those working in the nonprofit sector. This audience has a need for information on fund-raising, working with advisory boards, and recruitment of volunteers, for example, but has limited funds to travel to workshops around the country. Thus, the Learning Institute for Nonprofit Organizations, funded through the Kellogg Foundation, provides opportunities for nonprofit agencies to come together for working sessions in their local communities at sites in colleges, extension offices, and social service agencies. Workshops are offered via satellite and audioconferencing, with accompanying print-based materials and other resources available via CD-ROM and the World Wide Web. In highly interactive sessions, participants work collaboratively to master skills necessary for their individual organization's success and network with others who face similar challenges.

Concluding Comments

All in all, incorporating technology as an instructional strategy allows you to offer workshops to a potentially greater number and diversity of learners. Technology also allows use of a wider range of resource people, not only national and international speakers, but also the range of local experts who can enhance the resource pool. In addition, designing instruction to incorporate technology can provide opportunities for prolonged collaborative problem solving and enables learners to engage in new ways of teaching and learning. Although the tools are different for the delivery of workshops at a distance, many of the processes, including careful design, parallel those in face-to-face instruction. With appropriate technologies and support for instructors and learners, the learning outcomes more than justify the inputs of planning and support.

References

Apps, J. W., *Problems in Continuing Education*. San Francisco: Jossey-Bass, 1979.

Bates, A. W., *Technology, Open Learning and Distance Education*. New York: Routledge, 1995.

Cervero, R., and Wilson, A. *Planning Responsibly for Adult Education: A Guide to Negotiating Power and Interests*. San Francisco: Jossey-Bass, 1994.

Chute, A., Balthazar, L., and Poston, C. "Learning from Teletraining." In M. Moore and G. Clark (eds.), *Readings in Distance Learning and Instruction*, no. 2. University Park, Pa.: American Center for the Study of Distance Education, 1989.

Clark, R. "Reconsidering Research on Learning from Media." *Review of Educational Research*, 1983, 53, 450.

Cross, K. P. *Adults as Learners*. San Francisco: Jossey-Bass, 1981.

Dunning, B., Van Kekerix, M., and Zaborowski, L. *Reaching Learners Through Telecommunications*. San Francisco: Jossey-Bass, 1993.

Dutton, W., and Lievrouw, L. "Teleconferencing as an Educational Medium." In L. Parker, and C. Olgren (eds.), *Teleconferencing and Electronic Communications*. Madison: Center for Interactive Programs, University of Wisconsin-Extension, 1982.

Gibson, C. "Academic Self Concept—Its Nature and Import in Distance Education." *American Journal of Distance Education*, 1996, *10* (1), 23–36.

Gibson, T., and Gibson, C. (executive producers). *Quality Distance Education*. Madison: University of Wisconsin-Extension, 1995/96. Audio-, video- and computer-based instruction.

Ottoson, J. "After the Applause: Exploring Multiple Influences on Application Following an Adult Education Program." *Adult Education Quarterly*, 1997, 47 (2), 92–107.

Phelps, R., Wells, R., Ashworth, R., and Hahn, H. "Effectiveness and Costs of Distance Education Using Computer-Mediated Communication." *American Journal of Distance Education*, 1991, 5 (3), 7–19.

CHERE CAMPBELL GIBSON is associate professor and chair of the graduate program in continuing and vocational education at the University of Wisconsin–Madison.

TERRY L. GIBSON is director of program support at the University of Wisconsin–Extension and professor of continuing and vocational education at the University of Wisconsin–Madison.

Movement toward a comprehensive evaluation of learning has become
a top priority for all stakeholders—learners, providers, sponsors,
instructors, and certifying agents.

Workshop Evaluation: Old Myths and New Wisdom

Grover J. Andrews

The workshop has been a favorite delivery mode for short-term education for many decades, perhaps even centuries. Though the workshop of the past was significantly different in structure and form, its purpose of concentrated education has not changed. The informal environment of the past, however, has been replaced with a more rigorously structured learning experience that is outcome oriented. This change, in part, is a result of the national trend in this century toward accountability in all forms and levels of education. A widely used definition for a workshop today is that developed by the Commission on Colleges of the Southern Association of Colleges and Schools in 1971, which states that a "workshop usually meets for a continual period of time over a period of one or more days. The distinguishing feature of the workshop is that it combines instruction with laboratory or experimental activity for the participants. The emphasis is more likely to be on skill training than on general principles" (Southern Association of Colleges and Schools, 1977, p. 37). Several key elements present in this description of a workshop provide the framework for developing an appropriate evaluation and assessment plan: time, format, curriculum, methods. These elements are exhibited in how a workshop combines instruction with hands-on experience, often focuses largely on skill training, and is offered in a continuous format for a short period of time.

Evaluation plans for workshops should address each of these key elements and provide the specific outcomes data and feedback information needed by each of the stakeholders. Therefore, workshop evaluation must produce results that verify that the program has been successful and new skills have been learned that can be applied in an effective and efficient manner.

New Directions for Adult and Continuing Education, no. 76, Winter 1997   © Jossey-Bass Publishers   71

This chapter focuses on the effect of this trend toward increased accountability for workshop education and offers practical advice and resource examples for workshop evaluation. It begins with some of the early concerns about evaluating adults who learn (old myths); progresses through presentation of why to evaluate, types of evaluation, how to evaluate, and who evaluates; and concludes with practical principles and suggestions (new wisdom).

Old Myths

A number of old myths concerning the use of evaluation in educational programs for adults have existed over the years. Today, in some ways, they still exert an influence on evaluation and adult learning. Primary among these was the position of "let the buyer beware." If a workshop, course, or program was good enough, past participants will say so. If not, and buyers feel they wasted their money, so be it! No form of evaluation or accreditation was wanted or thought to be needed as a means of certifying quality for the buyer in advance. Since the majority of adult education programs were self-supporting from fees paid by the participants, it was felt that these learners should not be subjected to tests, examinations, or other end-of-course evaluations. This position was built on several myths from the eighteenth, nineteenth, and early twentieth centuries, including the notion that adult learning abilities diminish with age and the belief that adults would not return to the classroom if they had to take tests. It should be noted that early in this period, adult learners' needs were rather simple and usually had a single focus. Many were job- or task-oriented, and skill acquisition was verified by visually observing the learner in class or at work.

However, in the first half of the twentieth century, these myths began to fade. The work of psychologist E. L. Thorndike demonstrated that learning ability within itself does not lessen with age. In addition, the pioneering work of many adult educators, including that of Julius M. Nolte, dean of general extension at the University of Minnesota (as described by Drazek, Mitchell, Pyle, and Thompson, 1965), and Cyril O. Houle (1961), professor of education at the University of Chicago, demonstrated that adults will engage in serious learning for both personal enrichment and professional enhancement. Subsequent studies conducted in the second half of the twentieth century have further demonstrated and documented the changes in the world of adult learning in numbers involved, frequency of enrollment, and quality demands. In the early 1960s, J.W.C. Johnstone and R. J. Rivera (1965) found that approximately twenty-five million adults were engaging in at least one formal education course or program each year. In the early 1970s, Samuel B. Gould (1973) found in his national study of nontraditional education that nearly eighty million adults indicated a need for further learning. As cited in Peterson and Cross (1978), in the late 1970s Rexford Moon, director of Future Directions for a Learning Society Project of the College

Entrance Examination Board, indicated that, based on the results of their national study of the learning society, most adults in America had come to embrace the philosophy of lifelong learning and regularly engaged in some form of learning. Along with this philosophy of continuous learning also came a desire and demand for quality by the learner. Consequently, a pervasive theme that has emerged over the last three decades as a result of these and other studies is outcome assessment and performance documentation. The practice by workshop entrepreneurs of "let the buyer beware" is no longer acceptable. Adult learners now want and demand assurance of quality in advance and feedback on achievement throughout the activity. This is what workshop evaluation today is all about.

Why Evaluate?

As the nature and characteristics of adult learning and adult learners' needs have evolved from the simple to the complex throughout this century, so have both the need for and the methods of evaluation. For example, program planners today must have access to a comprehensive needs assessment that identifies all the stakeholders and their specific expectations in order to develop an evaluation process that will produce the information desired by each individual or group. Because the primary emphasis in workshops is frequently on job-related skill acquisition, the evaluation plan focuses on performance results. The many reasons and uses for evaluation can be categorized according to the users of the information: individual learner, learner-interested second parties (supervisors, employers, and so on), program developers, administrators, and certifying and regulatory agencies.

Individual Learners. Today individuals enroll in workshops for very specific purposes usually related to the need or desire to learn a new skill or improve on and update existing skills. They do this in response to current job- and work-related demands, for new career or position advancement, or for personal and avocational interests. Regardless of the reason, adult learners want reasonable assurance in advance that the workshop in which they enroll will provide them with the knowledge and skills they desire. A review of previous evaluation data on the quality of the workshop and the success of previous participants should provide the would-be learner with sufficient information to make enrollment decisions.

Learner-Interested Second Parties. In the past, it was a common practice by many employers to reward an employee by sending him or her to a continuing education workshop or conference, regardless of subject or topic. Today, the workshop attended must be focused and job related. Employers and supervisors of learners increasingly are requiring evaluation results that demonstrate that the expected outcomes from a workshop for their employees have been achieved. They want verification not only of required knowledge and skills but also of performance improvement back on the job.

Program Developers. The individuals responsible for developing the workshop program content and instructional methods must have the direct feedback on the success of their programs that evaluation results provide. Evaluation results on what works and what does not work in achieving the goals and objectives identified in the needs assessment enable the developer to make necessary improvements for future offerings of the same workshop. Results also provide valuable information for general use in future workshop development.

Administrators. General administrators of the organization responsible for the workshop need regular and frequent data for decision making on budget, personnel, materials, and other resource needs. Administrative decision making can no longer be made on one's "gut feelings" or personal bias. Organizational reengineering and reinvention must be based on a reliable, informational database of what works and who works with maximum efficiency. Administrative evaluation data is important for administrative accountability and for continuous improvement in the organization.

Certifying and Regulatory Agencies. If a workshop is to qualify participants for specific licensing, certifying, or funding sources, it must meet and maintain specified criteria and standards. Program developers must incorporate these needs into the workshop curriculum. Evaluation results should verify that they have been met and, if required, that the individual learner has achieved the learning outcomes specified for licensing or certification to practice.

Types of Evaluation

Based on the needs and purposes of evaluation previously discussed, four major types of workshop evaluation results should be produced: individual, program, organizational, and performance evaluations. Each has a very specific purpose and may be measured by separate or combined instruments and methods.

Individual. The assessment of individual learning goals and objectives is important in a workshop where the acquisition of knowledge and achievement of a certain level of performance is required for the individual employee by the employer; professional organization; or licensing, certifying, or accrediting agency. Personal achievement results are also important for the learners' self-assessment and motivation.

Program. Workshop program developers, administrators, and instructors need evaluation results in order to improve and maintain program quality. Instruction, curriculum, methods, skill experiences, and any other elements of the learning activity should be included in the evaluation process selected. Evaluation should provide accurate information on what was accomplished, what was not and why not, and what should be changed for future offerings.

Organizational. Evaluation results provide the organization's administrators with useful accountability data on the unit's overall effectiveness and efficiency. This type of data should be helpful to the principal decision makers of the organization as they determine structure, personnel, resource, space, materials, and equipment allocation.

Performance. Evaluation of learning outcomes and performance documentation provide the information on specific achievement levels that may be needed for the workshop to meet professional, licensing, certification, and regulatory agencies' requirements. It also enables the program administrator to know and promote this information about the workshop.

How to Evaluate

As workshop evaluation has become more complex, there has been a tendency for the process to become more visible to and intrusive on the learning process. Instead, every effort should be made to integrate the evaluation process into the learning process so that it is as nearly invisible as possible. Program developers should become like Charles Dickens's character the "Artful Dodger," who was successful in removing individuals' personal valuables without their knowledge, and so should program evaluations. They should enhance and not detract from the learning objectives of the workshop. Program planners should take care to ensure that the evaluation measures employed contribute to achieving the learning objectives of the workshop.

Essential to a successful evaluation is good program planning. (Sork presents new perspectives on planning in Chapter One.) The overall program plan should provide the basic information for determining the *who, what, when, where,* and *how* needed for both planning and evaluation. First, data from the needs assessment clearly identifies the learner target group and sharply focuses their specific learning needs. Once members of the target group and their specific needs have been identified, learning experiences can be designed that, if properly implemented, will achieve the desired learning outcomes. Consequently, how you evaluate totally depends on the program-planning process of *who* and *what.* These planning elements form the essential components of evaluation that deal with the individual learner and the substance of the subject matter of the workshop.

The *when, where,* and *how* of evaluation are primarily concerned with methods and techniques of evaluation and are also products of the planning process. The right method using the right techniques at just the right time is essential to collecting useful data and information and to evaluation's positive contribution to the educational process. For example, the end-of-workshop evaluation in which the instructor says, "On the way out, please pick up an evaluation form, fill it out, and drop it into a box in the hall or mail it back when you get home" is really sending the message that knowing what happened in this workshop is not very important. This message is verified by the low percentage of participants who normally respond to such an offer of evaluation. On the other hand, a carefully developed and planned use of an end-of-workshop evaluation form that has been integrated into the instructional component of the workshop can be very effective in determining customer satisfaction and for program improvement. This type of evaluation is usually very brief, but the questions are important. If the workshop instructor says at the conclusion, "The most important segment of the workshop is now at hand: your feedback on our success or failure," and talks the group through the questions before dismissal, a high percentage of meaningful responses can be obtained.

Workshops delivered by distant education methods provide a number of unique problems for evaluation. How do you evaluate and verify skill or knowledge acquisition by distant delivery modes? How do you know that the individual on the other end of the line participating in the evaluation is the person enrolled? How can you validate to employers and professional, certifying, and regulatory agencies that individual learning outcomes have been achieved? I am not aware of any technological solution to these questions to date. Current practice reverts to the old, and fairly reliable, technique of proctored exams or demonstrations in which the distant learner goes to a preapproved site for a face-to-face evaluation. Computer disk, video-computer- printer hookups, e-mail, and other technology-based experiments offer hope. I feel confident that in the near future a technologically based validating process that is reliable will be developed and utilized. (In Chapter Six, Gibson and Gibson raise additional questions associated with the use of instructional technology to provide education at a distance.)

Excellent examples of successful workshop and conference evaluation forms and techniques can be found in several source books. Three of the more useful resources are *Course Evaluations* (1993) and *The Best Evaluations for Seminars and Conferences* (1997), both published by the Learning Resource Network, and *The Continuing Education Guide* by Louis Phillips (1994).

Who Evaluates?

As previously discussed, evaluation of workshops today has become a multidimensional activity in which multiple stakeholders are interested. Evaluation of a single workshop could involve the instructor, the participant, the employer, the professional association, and other third parties. The task for the program administrator is to identify stakeholders in advance and to design the evaluation plan to meet the needs of each stakeholder. If it is not possible to integrate each interest into a process, every effort should be made to coordinate all evaluation needs into a single plan that enhances the learning experience and ensures that multiple evaluation activities are not dysfunctional in the learning process.

Instructor. Instructor evaluation is primarily concerned with measuring the learner's effectiveness in the acquisition of the knowledge and skills being taught in the workshop. This evaluation is tailored specifically to the material presented and has personal value to the clients.

Participant. The most commonly used evaluation format is the participant satisfaction survey. Usually this uses a standardized form at the end of the workshop and measures the participants' reactions to meeting arrangements (location, rooms, registration procedures, temperature, seating, living accommodations, and food) and general opinions about the program (instructor, materials, schedule, usefulness of the course, future needs). These data inform both the program planner and the organizational administrator about the overall efficiency of the operations. They have little value for the clients.

Employer or Professional. The participant's employer and professional organizations increasingly are seeking accountability feedback on the educational activities of the individual employee or member. Employer interest centers primarily in two areas: employee's work-related skill acquisition and effective use of employer training dollars. Professional organizations are interested in updating skills to improve professional competence and practice and to meet membership, certification, and licensing requirements. This evaluation is of great value to the client.

Third Party. An individual participant in a workshop may have additional stakeholders or a third party who is interested in the evaluation results of their learning activities. It is important that the program developer make every effort to identify stakeholders at the time of the needs assessment and target group identification. By so doing, the planner can accommodate third-party needs by designing the right evaluation scheme in the planning process. This is particularly true for groups or organizations that may be tangentially related at the time of the workshop but to whom the mastery of the materials or skills offered may transfer to meet a similar requirement. A precise identification of these needs will enable the program designer to tailor evaluations to produce those results that will encourage multiple uses of workshop learning. Currently, the transfer use (or acceptance) of knowledge or skills learned in one setting for a specific purpose has not been readily accepted by another group who was not directly involved in the planning, design, and implementation of the program. Early identification of third-party groups and their early involvement in the program can help to remedy this situation. This evaluation can be of great value to the client.

Practice, Principles, and Guidelines for Successful Evaluation

Throughout this chapter it has been emphasized that evaluation is a pervasive component in program planning. Evaluation must not be an addendum to the overall learning experience. Evaluation questions should be developed for each major workshop and program segment. Program planners should develop an evaluation consciousness that will be present throughout the whole program-planning cycle. The concepts on planning, assessment, and evaluation presented in the *Principles of Good Practice in Continuing Education*

Figure 7.1. An Integrated Planning and Evaluation Process

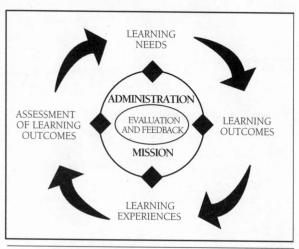

Source: Adapted from *Principles of Good Practice in Continuing Education* (International Association for Continuing Education and Training, 1983, p. 4). Used by permission.

developed by the International Association for Continuing Education and Training (1983) provide a framework for achieving an integrated approach to workshop planning and evaluation.

In this model, evaluation and feedback occur throughout each step in program planning, thus enabling the administrator, the program developer, the instructional staff, and the various stakeholders to receive data and make informed decisions throughout. This basic principle allows for improvements and changes to be made as appropriate before the workshop takes place. The figure presents a cyclical process that progresses from conducting a needs assessment, to writing learning outcomes, to creating the appropriate learning experiences through instructional design, to assessing the achievement of learning outcomes. Evaluation of each step in the cycle provides feedback for improvement of the process.

Another guiding principle relates specifically to the *assessment of learning outcomes* component of the integrated planning and evaluation process presented in Figure 7.1. Based on the results of the planning activities involved in determining learning needs, learning outcomes, and learning experiences, the major emphasis in developing the evaluation plan is to select the appropriate methods and techniques for assessing learning outcomes. The International Association for Continuing Education and Training (1991) developed and published *A Practical Handbook for Assessing Learning Outcomes in Continuing Education and Training*. This publication contains a continuum of ten possible assessment plans ranging from the very simple to the very complex (see Figure 7.2).

Figure 7.2. Practical Guide to Assessment Plans

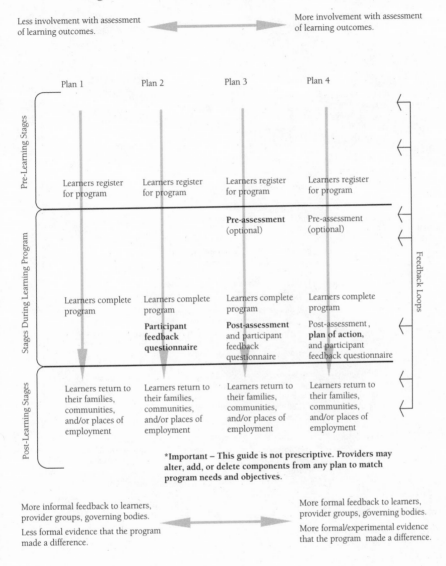

Less involvement with assessment of learning outcomes.

More involvement with assessment of learning outcomes.

Pre-Learning Stages

Stages During Learning Program

Post-Learning Stages

Feedback Loops

Plan 1	Plan 2	Plan 3	Plan 4
Learners register for program	Learners register for program	Learners register for program	Learners register for program
		Pre-assessment (optional)	Pre-assessment (optional)
Learners complete program	Learners complete program	Learners complete program	Learners complete program
	Participant feedback questionnaire	**Post-assessment** and participant feedback questionnaire	Post-assessment, **plan of action,** and participant feedback questionnaire
Learners return to their families, communities, and/or places of employment	Learners return to their families, communities, and/or places of employment	Learners return to their families, communities, and/or places of employment	Learners return to their families, communities, and/or places of employment

*Important – This guide is not prescriptive. Providers may alter, add, or delete components from any plan to match program needs and objectives.

More informal feedback to learners, provider groups, governing bodies.

Less formal evidence that the program made a difference.

More formal feedback to learners, provider groups, governing bodies.

More formal/experimental evidence that the program made a difference.

Figure 7.2. Practical Guide to Assessment Plans (*Continued*)

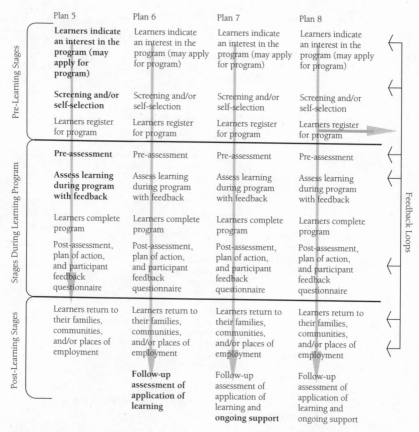

Less involvement with assessment of learning outcomes.

More involvement with assessment of learning outcomes.

	Plan 5	Plan 6	Plan 7	Plan 8
Pre-Learning Stages	**Learners indicate an interest in the program (may apply for program)**	Learners indicate an interest in the program (may apply for program)	Learners indicate an interest in the program (may apply for program)	Learners indicate an interest in the program (may apply for program)
	Screening and/or self-selection	Screening and/or self-selection	Screening and/or self-selection	Screening and/or self-selection
	Learners register for program	Learners register for program	Learners register for program	Learners register for program
Stages During Learning Program	**Pre-assessment**	Pre-assessment	Pre-assessment	Pre-assessment
	Assess learning during program with feedback	Assess learning during program with feedback	Assess learning during program with feedback	Assess learning during program with feedback
	Learners complete program	Learners complete program	Learners complete program	Learners complete program
	Post-assessment, plan of action, and participant feedback questionnaire	Post-assessment, plan of action, and participant feedback questionnaire	Post-assessment, plan of action, and participant feedback questionnaire	Post-assessment, plan of action, and participant feedback questionnaire
Post-Learning Stages	Learners return to their families, communities, and/or places of employment	Learners return to their families, communities, and/or places of employment	Learners return to their families, communities, and/or places of employment	Learners return to their families, communities, and/or places of employment
		Follow-up assessment of application of learning	Follow-up assessment of application of learning and **ongoing support**	Follow-up assessment of application of learning and ongoing support

Feedback Loops

More informal feedback to learners, provider groups, governing bodies.

Less formal evidence that the program made a difference.

More formal feedback to learners, provider groups, governing bodies.

More formal/experimental evidence that the program made a difference.

Less involvement with assessment of learning outcomes.

More involvement with assessment of learning outcomes.

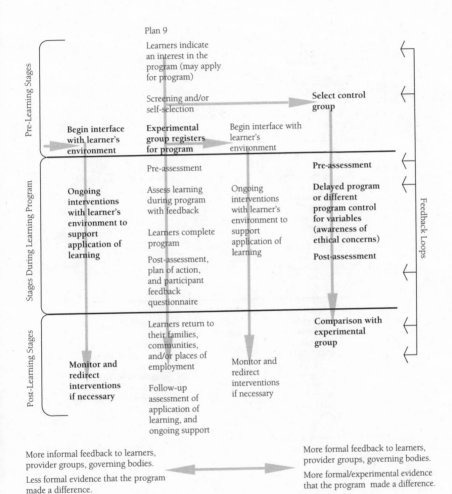

Plan 9

Pre-Learning Stages

Learners indicate an interest in the program (may apply for program)

Screening and/or self-selection

Select control group

Begin interface with learner's environment

Experimental group registers for program

Begin interface with learner's environment

Stages During Learning Program

Pre-assessment

Pre-assessment

Ongoing interventions with learner's environment to support application of learning

Assess learning during program with feedback

Learners complete program

Post-assessment, plan of action, and participant feedback questionnaire

Ongoing interventions with learner's environment to support application of learning

Delayed program or different program control for variables (awareness of ethical concerns)

Post-assessment

Feedback Loops

Post-Learning Stages

Learners return to their families, communities, and/or places of employment

Follow-up assessment of application of learning, and ongoing support

Monitor and redirect interventions if necessary

Monitor and redirect interventions if necessary

Comparison with experimental group

More informal feedback to learners, provider groups, governing bodies.

Less formal evidence that the program made a difference.

More formal feedback to learners, provider groups, governing bodies.

More formal/experimental evidence that the program made a difference.

Figure 7.2. Practical Guide to Assessment Plans (*Continued*)

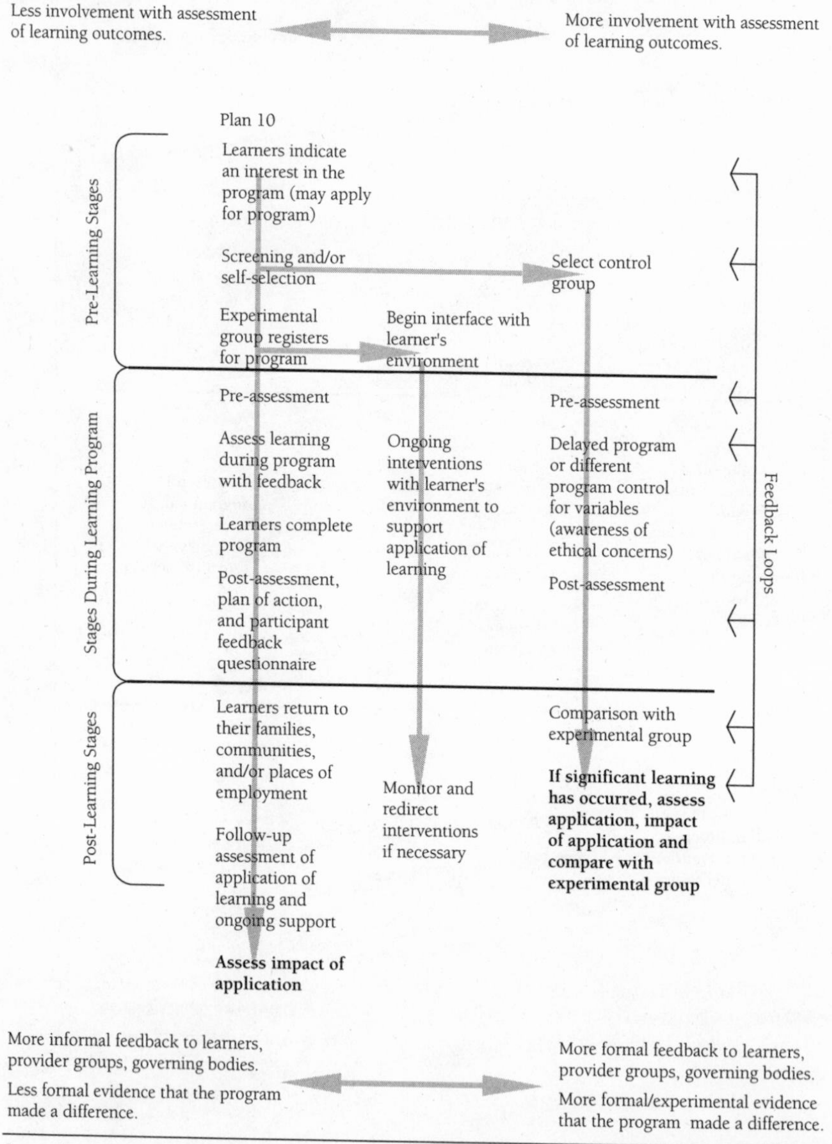

Less involvement with assessment
of learning outcomes.

More involvement with assessment
of learning outcomes.

Pre-Learning Stages

Plan 10

Learners indicate
an interest in the
program (may apply
for program)

Screening and/or
self-selection

Select control
group

Experimental
group registers
for program

Begin interface with
learner's
environment

Stages During Learning Program

Pre-assessment

Assess learning
during program
with feedback

Ongoing
interventions
with learner's
environment to
support
application of
learning

Learners complete
program

Post-assessment,
plan of action,
and participant
feedback
questionnaire

Pre-assessment

Delayed program
or different
program control
for variables
(awareness of
ethical concerns)

Post-assessment

Feedback Loops

Post-Learning Stages

Learners return to
their families,
communities,
and/or places of
employment

Monitor and
redirect
interventions
if necessary

Comparison with
experimental group

Follow-up
assessment of
application of
learning and
ongoing support

**If significant learning
has occurred, assess
application, impact
of application and
compare with
experimental group**

**Assess impact of
application**

More informal feedback to learners,
provider groups, governing bodies.

Less formal evidence that the program
made a difference.

More formal feedback to learners,
provider groups, governing bodies.

More formal/experimental evidence
that the program made a difference.

Source: International Association for Continuing Education and Training, 1992. Used by permission.

An "Assessment Plan Decision Survey" is also included in the handbook. This instrument guides the planner in selecting and creating the best outcome assessment plan for the learning activity, beginning in the very first stages of the program-planning process. This model is also available on a computer disk. It should be noted that the processes included in the various plans are interchangeable, thus enabling the program developer to adapt the evaluation to the specific needs and objectives of a specific workshop or program. The guidebook also contains an extensive compendium of evaluation questions to draw upon. The questions are arranged in categories: presenter and methods, course content, participant benefits, course setting, and overall. Each is keyed to the ten assessment plans.

Successful workshop evaluations depend on careful planning and coordination of each step in the overall planning process. The key points of evaluation offered by Phillips (1994) are excellent guideposts for the workshop planner to benchmark: (1) have a specific purpose in mind for your evaluation, (2) do not include an evaluation question (activity) unless you can do something about the results from that question, (3) alternate evaluation methods periodically to look at data from different perspectives, (4) focus evaluation efforts on the weakest areas of program development and delivery, (5) make evaluation an integral part of program planning, not an afterthought, (6) connect your program evaluation with your needs assessment and learning outcomes, and (7) keep it simple. I add an eighth guidepost: (8) integrate the evaluation throughout the program in an invisible and unobtrusive manner that enhances learning. Phillips also includes evaluation guidelines and sample evaluation forms and questions.

New Wisdom—A Postscript

After a hundred years we have moved a long way from the old myths of adult learning. Their somewhat negative influence, which inhibited the use of meaningful evaluations and quality assurance measures in workshops and adult learning activities, have been replaced with new knowledge and positive attitudes. A long progression of research, field tests, and new learning experiences has led to new wisdom that is more positive about how and why adults learn and why today they more aggressively engage in continuous learning throughout life. As society has changed during this century, the educational needs of the workforce of the nation have changed. This transition has paralleled the societal shifts from agriculture to industry to service and technology. With each of these societal transitions, the individual's educational and skill needs to obtain and retain a job or profession have significantly increased. There is no longer an "education for life." Rather, for today, and for tomorrow, there is a need for education throughout one's life. This new wisdom from learners and educators became evident in the research conducted by IACET in the early 1990s, summarized in its *Assessment of Learning Outcomes in Continuing Education and Training: A Status Study* (1992).

In its national survey of educational organizations, professional associations, health care organizations, business and industry, and government agencies, IACET found that "the general public is beginning to view continuing education as a means of personal growth and fulfillment," and "Indeed, adults are progressively viewing lifelong learning as a fundamental tool for improving the quality, and perhaps even quantity, of the experience called life" (p. 12). Research data show that a majority of the respondents (over 90 percent) believe that assessing learning outcomes enhances the quality of continuing education and training. In other words, during the past century we have moved dramatically from a position of saying *no* to evaluations for adult learning activities to a position of saying *yes*. Adult learners have moved from a position of fearing assessment and evaluation in their learning activities to one of demanding assessment of learning outcomes and verification of quality.

Therefore, the new wisdom seems to say that adults today aggressively engage in learning throughout life for both personal and professional reasons, they want reasonable assurance of quality in their learning activities prior to enrolling, and they want documentation on competence and skill performance. As continuing educators and program developers, we must learn to deliver and evaluate our programs within the parameters of the new wisdom. We must be accountable.

References

The Best Evaluations for Seminars and Conferences. Learning Resources Network (LERN) Research Report No. 02–666. Manhattan, Kans.: Learning Resources Network, 1997.

Course Evaluations. Learning Resources Network (LERN) Research Report No. 013. Manhattan, Kans.: Learning Resources Network, 1993.

Drazek, S. J., Mitchell, N. P., Pyle, H. G., and Thompson, W. L. *Expanding Horizons . . . Continuing Education.* Washington, D.C.: National University Extension Association, 1965.

Gould, S. B. *Diversity by Design.* San Francisco: Jossey-Bass, 1973.

Houle, C. O. *The Inquiring Mind.* Madison: University of Wisconsin Press, 1961.

International Association for Continuing Education and Training. *Principles of Good Practice in Continuing Education.* Washington, D.C.: IACET, 1983.

International Association for Continuing Education and Training. *A Practical Handbook for Assessing Learning Outcomes in Continuing Education and Training.* Washington, D.C.: IACET, 1991.

International Association for Continuing Education and Training. *Assessment of Learning Outcomes in Continuing Education and Training: A Status Study.* Washington, D.C.: IACET, 1992.

Johnstone, J.W.C., and Rivera, R. J. *Volunteers for Learning: A Study of Educational Pursuits.* Chicago: Aldine, 1965.

Peterson, R. E., and Cross, K. P. *Toward a Lifelong Learning in America: A Sourcebook for Planners.* Vol. 37. Berkeley: Educational Testing Service, 1978.

Phillips, L. *The Continuing Education Guide: The CEU and Other Professional Development Criteria.* Dubuque, Iowa: Kendall/Hunt, 1994.

Southern Association of Colleges and Schools. *Standards of the College Delegate Assembly.* Atlanta, Ga.: Commission on Colleges, Southern Association of Colleges and Schools, 1977.

GROVER J. ANDREWS is associate director for instructional services at the Center for Continuing Education and adjunct faculty at the Department of Adult Education, College of Education, at the University of Georgia in Athens.

This chapter provides a practitioner's reflections on planning and facilitating workshops and her perspectives on some of the major themes discussed in other chapters in this sourcebook.

Confessions of a Workshop-aholic

Doe Hentschel

A week after delivering "The Development and Implementation of a Simulation Workshop as a Strategy for Changing Job Behaviors of Adult Education Administrators" (Hentschel, 1979) to my dissertation committee, I called them to touch base before the hearing. "I have just one problem, Doe," warned the evaluation expert on the committee. "You keep using that dumb adult education word, 'facilitate.' You *directed* the workshop. You *taught* the participants. And I have a Ph.D. and you don't, so what do you plan to do?"

I took a deep breath, thought about the consequences of my choices, and responded without hesitation. "I'm going to change the words 'facilitate' and 'facilitator' wherever they appear. Then I'm going to get my Ph.D. and explain to you why you are wrong."

And I did. That conversation happened nearly twenty years ago. The manuscript conversion predated the miracle of word processing and was no easy task. More important, what my professor saw as a semantic attempt of a marginalized group of educators to stake out their claim to disciplinary recognition by developing their own jargon is really a different approach to teaching and learning that deserves validation.

In the intervening years and throughout many rich and enriching experiences as a professor, an administrator of adult and continuing education, vice president of a liberal arts college, a consultant, and a facilitator for zillions of programs, I confess to never once believing that *facilitating* was just a "dumb adult education word." I confess to, more often than not, designing and facilitating workshops rather than directing and teaching traditional classes. I confess to considering lectures as a last resort for *facilitating* (there it is!) learning. I confess to believing that if the learners don't get it (and ideally they and I know and agree on the antecedent of *it*), there must be something more or different *I* can do to make it possible for them to accomplish their goals. And I

NEW DIRECTIONS FOR ADULT AND CONTINUING EDUCATION, no. 76, Winter 1997 © Jossey-Bass Publishers

confess to proselytizing about the worth of facilitating, to advocating for instructional designs that demand talented facilitation, and to self-consciously demonstrating and modeling, whenever possible and to the best of my abilities, effective facilitation skills.

So, what does a self-avowed, unabashedly biased addict of workshops have to contribute to a sourcebook on the best current thinking and practice about this special kind of program and learning? This chapter combines reactions to the principles, tenets, and suggestions of my author colleagues with more confessions and examples from those zillion workshops I have facilitated.

Confessions About Workshop Planning

One of the biggest challenges I face in planning and facilitating workshops, typically with colleagues who are not formally trained adult educators, is to get them to plan. Administrative types want to jump from "Let's have a workshop" to "The brochure needs to be mailed by February 15." Cofacilitators are more inclined to jump to "Let's run it for two days and begin with an icebreaker 9:00 A.M." No one on the planning committee wants a lecture on program planning, but they are making horrendous and unexamined assumptions about the client system, the potential participants, the desired outcomes, and every other aspect of program planning. Minimally, I should whip out this sourcebook and require my colleagues to study it carefully. In reality, that is not going to happen. I would risk being labeled an obstructionist or worse if I attempted to get the group to follow thoughtful and systematic program-planning practices. They think they know how to do it and would resent my belaboring the deficiencies in their process or lack thereof.

I confess, therefore, to being a closet planner. I typically do my planning before and after the "planning" meeting just described so that most of the appropriate analysis happens. If I am fortunate enough to be facilitating the meeting (sorry for redundancy in my vocabulary, but an addict is an addict), I can structure the discussion so that the group cannot avoid the basics of the process. But, by and large, I do my planning in private rather than intrude on the group process with what would most likely be viewed as a theoretical exercise with little relevance to what should happen when the unidentified participants arrive at the cleverly titled workshop to learn something-or-other.

Lest you think I am the only living, breathing example of a practitioner who always does it right, however, let me confess that there are times when I do not follow a systematic planning process. Furthermore, I always knew that the real world does not work the way the models imply. As a professor, I discovered that many of my graduate students had little or no experience designing programs. Some of those students actually thought memorizing the models and steps in their textbooks would guarantee their success as program planners.

Having come through the more traditional back door, I knew better. My solution was to design a (you guessed it!) workshop in which the class members planned and ran a self-supporting workshop as a professional development program for adult education practitioners.

Anne Will, who clarifies the difference between collaborative and cooperative learning in her chapter "Group Learning in Workshops," would recognize this experience as truly collaborative. I served as a resource, but many times the class ventured into unknown territory only to discover a truth that even I had not anticipated. They lamented the amount of time spent discussing menus, discovered the realities of making programmatic choices based on fiscal resources, confronted a bureaucracy that thwarted every model they had studied, and celebrated their own inventiveness as they learned which corners to cut to meet deadlines. They also learned the rewards of good planning. Howard McCluskey, in one of his last public appearances, complimented the class by telling the workshop participants that never in his career had he had so clear an understanding of who the audience would be, what the goals of the workshop were, and what was expected of him as a featured speaker. Several of those in attendance who had had the privilege of previously hearing him observed that this presentation was one of the best ever made by this trailblazer in our profession.

After decades of practice I confess to believing that understanding the gestalt of the planning process is more important than the model of the moment or the sequential steps we might or might not follow. I often ignore some of the basic steps (and thank you, Thomas Sork, for recognizing that some of our most cherished elements such as needs assessment and stating objectives can be limiting). Sometimes I mix up the order of those steps. And sometimes I just trust my intuition, which is, after all, born not only of inspiration and insight but also of experiences I have reflected on and therefore learned from.

Confessions About Outcomes and Evaluation

In their chapters on workshop planning and evaluation, Sork and Andrews discuss the importance of clarifying intended outcomes. I believe that a truly talented facilitator will also work hard to anticipate unintended outcomes. I think that is the best way to ensure that the intended outcomes are achieved *and* prepare for the unpredictable process issues that Sork mentions. If a workshop is truly interactive, there will always be some unintended issues and outcomes as the participants contribute their own experiences, talents, skills, and strengths and inject their biases, limitations, and demands. The facilitator needs to be able to use those contributions appropriately and to avoid the surprise of running headlong into a barrier thrown in by a participant.

I once designed a simulation workshop as a module for a graduate course titled "Leadership for Change," which I was teaching in a weekend format. The goal was for the students to understand how people in organizations deal with change and how organizational structures and systems can aid or impede change processes. My brilliant plan was to have the class role-play a company on a government contract that would design models for educational change in three different learning environments. While the class member I had appointed as president met with those she had hired as department heads during the opening session on Friday night, I took the role of the human resource director and gave the other class members employment applications to complete. I also explained the work rules of the company, which immediately conveyed to the class members that the informal, relaxed culture established in previous meetings was now a more rigid and regulated environment.

All day Saturday, I intruded in the work of the company to inject more changes designed to create stress and conflict. Morale progressed in the predictable direction. When the deadline for completion was accelerated by a full month to the following morning, panic set in, accompanied by anger and frustration. I found myself cast in the role of support staff for all three departments. Assuming (incorrectly) that the project required written reports, they demanded typewriters, ditto masters (which dates this experience!), and someone (guess who) to run off twenty-three copies of everything they produced. By the end of the day I was as miserable as they were!

Sunday morning arrived, and the three departments presented their innovative and insightful reports. Then we began the more important task of processing the experience. Suddenly, one class member blurted out, "We should all flunk this course! We're here to learn how to be change agents, but none of us did anything to bring about change. We just went right along and did what we were told to do and griped about it every step of the way." The president admitted she knew how unhappy everyone was but was afraid to stop the work to explore what was wrong because she wanted to be sure the organization finished its work. After all, she wanted to get a good grade in the course and being a "good president" would contribute to that.

As authorities on the power dynamics in the learning environment, Johnson-Bailey and Cervero might have anticipated this outcome, but I had not. What we had experienced was a simulated organization operating *within* a real organization with a real power structure. As professor, I was perceived to hold power over the students, just as the boss in a real organization does, and no one was willing to risk the consequences of not doing what the "boss" had directed.

In final course evaluations (which were extremely positive) most of the students commented that the simulation was one of the most powerful learning experiences of their lives. Years later, a member of that class reiterated its importance and how she had applied that learning when she became a college president. I must confess, however, that although I taught that same seminar for several years, I never repeated the simulation. The alienation I felt from the students that weekend and their anger and frustration were so painful to me that I could not submit another class or myself to it again. Maybe I am a coward. Maybe I am pathologically dependent on the approval of others. Or maybe this was an ethical choice for me that had to do with use and abuse of power. I have not decided, but I still feel the emotion of that weekend as if it were yesterday.

Andrews's chapter reminds me of some unfinished work of mine. As part of my doctoral research, I developed a simulation workshop in which practitioners learned and applied a specific evaluation model. I then researched the outcomes of that workshop on participants' knowledge, attitudes, and skills. In what some described as the ultimate Tylerian approach, I actually measured those skills one year after the workshop was completed (Hentschel, 1979).

My next serious research project was to revisit the experimental group two years later to determine whether the significant changes I had observed after one year continued over a longer term (Hentschel, 1980). The results puzzled me greatly. Participants still claimed to have learned a great deal about evaluation, and most identified the workshop as the critical intervention where they developed their skills. In practice, however, they were using fewer of the specific steps of the evaluation model they were taught than they had two years before the workshop!

I struggled for an explanation of this apparent paradox and found it in my understanding of adult learning. When we measure learning against our own intended outcomes, no matter how carefully and thoroughly we clarify them and plan with those outcomes in mind, we are leaving out of the equation the impact of the adult learners' motivations, needs, experiences, previous skills, attitudes, and creativity. Learners will of course modify what they have been taught as they integrate that learning into their regular lives. Every change agent recognizes that challenge, and as workshop designers and facilitators, we too are trying to change behaviors or attitudes. It seems to me that the more experience learners have in using the innovations they learn in the workshop, the more likely they are to modify the skills they learned. The result is that their demonstrated skills over time look less and less like what we thought they would look like when we planned the workshop. Does it mean they did not learn what they were supposed to learn in the workshop? Of course not! But it does mean that a strict, outcomes-based (Tylerian) approach is terribly limiting if we are interested in *measuring* the impact of the workshop over time.

My life moved in a different direction at that point in time, and I confess to abandoning the search for a way to evaluate that long-term impact. It is still an important issue, however, to all the stakeholders that Andrews identifies.

Confessions About Learning in Groups

My very first group project in my first graduate class was designing "How Adults Learn in Groups," a workshop to train facilitators. I was not yet an addict, but I had sampled and tested group facilitation enough to know that group learning was exhilarating. This project helped me learn how to achieve that thrill predictably. I still use materials from that workshop, and the things I learned in developing it are so deeply embedded in my philosophy and practice that they have become instinctive.

Will and other authors in this volume provide many guidelines for adult learning in groups. I would suggest that facilitators free themselves up from viewing those rules as restrictive absolutes. I was once asked to perform a miracle in workshop facilitation. The request was for an interactive workshop to break down stereotypical attitudes and build better relationships between collegiates and alumnae members of my national sorority. The intended outcome was for the participants to leave the workshop with specific "collumnae" programs that they could implement in their own chapters. When I feebly suggested that these were impossible goals given the size of the group (seven hundred) and its diversity (ages from twenty to seventy, from all over North America), the immediate response was, "Well, we'll give you all afternoon in the large ballroom!"

Eighteen years later, that three-hour convention session is a legend in Delta Gamma. It resulted in over a hundred well-designed program plans for collumnae activities, which were published in a handbook that remained in use for at least ten years. My cofacilitator (who became a lifelong friend and professional collaborator) and I "planned backwards" from those outcomes; drew on our extensive knowledge and understanding of group dynamics, adult learning theory, and psychology; and most important, cared about the participants and what would happen to and with them during the workshop.

Effective facilitators know their group members and view them as unique individuals (even when there are seven hundred of them that they have never met). They select appropriate activities for the group based on who the group members are, what they need to learn, and how they will be comfortable learning. They guide, they listen, and they give feedback and suggestions. They offer respect, support, and empathy. They model effective group behaviors, and they are honest. Effective facilitators expect to learn from the participants, just as they take responsibility for designing a workshop that will enable the participants to learn.

These are very different responsibilities from those of the teacher defined as the knowledgeable expert who controls all the dynamics of the learning environment. Empowering learners is threatening to most teachers, at least in part because it feels like an abdication of responsibility (Hentschel and Hilton, 1983). The biggest leap one must take in learning to design and facilitate workshops is to believe that the teacher can and should be a learner. Becoming self-reflective about one's own learning when one's identity is based on subject matter expertise is unsettling, to say the least. In my experience with college faculty, I found that even those who espouse values of active learning and collaboration are uncomfortable with critical self-reflection and self-disclosure as advocated by Brookfield (1995). If faculty adopt this new self-concept, it transforms the very nature of the academy (Hentschel and Thompson, 1997).

This kind of transformation of self is not the likely result of reading an article (or even a whole sourcebook). It will not follow a dynamic lecture or even a whole course about teaching and learning. It *might* happen in an intensive, residential workshop if, in addition to the detachment and continuity described by Bersch and Fleming, there is also group support (both during and after the workshop) for changing the culture in which the self operates. The systems in which we live and work can exert tremendous power to protect the status quo (Cervero, 1985). No matter how potent our personal epiphany, when we return to our "real" world, the epiphany frequently fades.

When I reflect on a lifetime of residential workshops, I wonder what made the difference between those that truly changed my thinking, my values, and therefore my life and those that served as interesting, welcome, but not necessarily transformational respites. The question is more than a philosophical inquiry because I am currently embarking on an entrepreneurial venture to develop quality-of-life retreat workshops for women. How key is the location or the length of the workshop to helping each woman identify, explore, and ultimately change those aspects of her life that she feels are detracting from the quality she seeks? What role does the group play in that process? Is the primary element the woman herself—who she is, where she is in her life, the choices she herself makes? What can and *must* I, as planner and facilitator, do to support and encourage those choices?

Confessions About My Motivation

A few years after I left full-time teaching to become a dean, I reflected on my feelings about teaching, which I continue to do as often as possible. I wrote,

> It's the first night of a new semester, and . . . my own fatigue dissipates miraculously. . . . There's a special energy here—it simultaneously flows from me and to me as I feel a group being born. . . . I am again a teacher. A facilitator. A co-learner. I want to do cartwheels and flips! . . . [W]hat seems to me to make this moment work has little to do with the stuff we use to fashion adult education into a respectable discipline. What's happening here, what brings me back [again and again], is almost plain, unadulterated emotion. . . . I know I am in this classroom because it is constantly engaging, constantly challenging and constantly rewarding in ways which no other work I have ever done has ever been. I know that I do it the way I do it because it feels good this way. And I know if I stop caring it will not matter how much research I have done, read or published—I will no longer be any good at it. (Hentschel, 1985, p. 2)

At the risk of being accused of being overly zealous, I confess that I believe that all the planning, assessing, analyzing, and designing we do are of secondary importance to the interpersonal dynamics during the workshop. Those dynamics are never as predictable as our planning would imply. Much like the playwright, director, set designer, and choreographer, the planners must finally turn it over to the facilitator who, like the actor, will breathe life into the design. The facilitator needs more than a well-written and well-rehearsed script. The facilitator must have energy, talent, sensitivity, and passion if the workshop is to live. There are those who may label that statement a "dumb adult education idea." But I got my Ph.D. a long time ago, and I will happily defend my words as passionately as I facilitate workshops!

References

Brookfield, S. D. *Becoming a Critically Reflective Teacher.* San Francisco: Jossey-Bass, 1995.

Cervero, R. M. "Continuing Professional Education and Behavioral Change: A Model for Research and Evaluation." *Journal of Continuing Education in Nursing,* 1985, *16,* 85–88.

Hentschel, D. "The Development and Implementation of a Simulation Workshop as a Strategy for Changing Job Behaviors of Adult Education Administrators." Unpublished doctoral dissertation, School of Education, University of Wisconsin–Milwaukee, 1979.

Hentschel, D. "Long-Term Effectiveness of a Simulation Workshop as a Strategy for Increasing Knowledge and Changing Job Behaviors of Adult Education Administrators." In *Lifelong Learning Research Conference Proceedings.* College Park: Department of Agriculture and Extension Education, University of Maryland, 1980.

Hentschel, D. "Perspectives." *Lifelong Learning: An Omnibus of Practice and Research,* 1985, *9* (3), 2.

Hentschel, D., and Hilton, R. J. "Teaching Tips: From Terror to Empowerment." *Learning Connection,* 1983, *4* (5), 13.

Hentschel, D., and Thompson, S. G. "Transforming a College—Transforming Ourselves." In Proceedings: *The Learning Paradigm Conference.* San Marcos, Calif.: Palomar College, 1997.

DOE HENTSCHEL *is president of DBK Enterprises, Incorporated, which specializes in innovative program design.*

The workshop is being seen in different ways that are affecting
planning, design, and evaluation practices now and for the future.

The Workshop Through New Eyes

Jean Anderson Fleming

> The real voyage of discovery consists not in seeking new landscapes
> but in having new eyes.
>
> Marcel Proust

In the beginning pages of this volume, I used the metaphor of the workhorse to describe the workshop in our practice of adult and continuing education. The workshop has been around since time immemorial, it seems,
and, even when used only in the purest sense of the term, it seems to be
every place we look. We depend on the workshop to help adults learn what
they need to know for their professional and personal lives. We expect it to
be an interactive format and to last a relatively short period of time. We have
almost come to take the workshop for granted, planning and conducting by
rote formula. The ways in which the authors of this sourcebook view the
workshop, however, suggest a greater depth, complexity, and potential
beyond the technical how-to of workshop design. Their perspectives reflect
adult and continuing educators' awareness of the need for ethically responsible practice that incorporates current thinking on adult development and
learning, program planning, and evaluation. By looking at workshops with
new eyes, these experienced educators are able not only to describe methods and techniques but also to provide frameworks for critically examining
workshops to determine how well we respect the needs, wants, and rights
of adult learners.

    As authors have looked anew at workshops, however, they have seen
the need to address the questions of how well we actually conduct them.
This examination ranges from the most intense questions of negotiating
power dynamics to the critical questions of answering stakeholders' needs

for assessment data and feedback. The authors hope that readers felt challenged to examine their own philosophies and practices by using the insights provided in these chapters.

The overall intent of this sourcebook was to provide an updated look at the design and implementation of effective workshops. *Updated* means that workshops were to be examined in light of current contexts and, as Sork states in his chapter, in light of new understandings and sensitivities about planning, education, and learning. As Proust suggests, seeking new landscapes is not needed: the workshop remains a valuable educational format. Looking at it with new eyes, however, allows us to discover and act on social, political, economic, and organizational influences. A new perspective also allows us to see more clearly the varied potentials of workshops, from learning in residence to education at a distance.

As I reviewed how authors depicted workshops in this sourcebook, I kept returning to two major concerns: the contexts of both the workshop and the adult learner, and the diverse potential of this one educational format. Discussions of each follow, based on major ideas from the previous eight chapters. I have raised questions based on each author's work with which we can begin to examine the ethics and effectiveness of our own practice.

Context

In the first chapter, Sork set the tone for the remainder of this sourcebook. He introduced a three-dimensional model for educational design, the use of which is guided by a question-based approach to planning. As Sork explains, the third dimension delves into the concerns that lurk below the technical level of workshop planning, while his use of questions acknowledges the unique character of every planning situation. He acknowledges the contributions of Cervero and Wilson on the negotiation of social and political influences on the planning process. He goes on, however, to address the ethical dimension of planning, wherein the difficult, moral questions need to be asked. The questions raised by Sork lead us to examine not only our approach to workshop design but also our own epistemological and philosophical orientations toward planning and education. The challenge is for readers to act on ensuing insights.

Focusing on the life contexts of adult learners heightens our awareness not only of contextual influences but also of the individual learner as a person. An individual's perspectives and feelings become almost tangible when we choose to honor that person's real-life contexts and social identity. Johnson-Bailey and Cervero, for example, bring to our awareness the impact of social hierarchies and power relationships on the learning environment. The questions we must ask relate to our knowledge of and our willingness and ability to negotiate the power dynamics that are played out in our workshops. These concerns seem to be particularly important when one considers the intense and interactive nature of effective workshops.

Our responsibility to honor an individual's life context and history is again heightened through Wlodkowski's work. He explains that human motivation is inseparable from culture and then focuses on the central role of intrinsic motivation in learning. I believe Wlodkowski would have us ask ourselves to decide how well we design workshops to evoke and sustain the intrinsic motivation of learners and ensure opportunity for full participation by all people.

Andrews draws our attention to the contexts of the workshop itself. He emphasizes our responsibility to provide the data and feedback required by the myriad stakeholders of adult learning endeavors. The demand is for accountability; workshops must produce results, and we must be able to provide proof of those results. The question is, How well do we provide assessment of learning outcomes and verification of quality to learners, program developers, certifying agencies, employers, and other interested parties? Considered carefully, this question goes to the heart of ensuring ethically responsible practice.

Potential

We have long recognized the potential of workshops, yet there are new dimensions being realized in response to new developments and needs of current times. Gibson and Gibson, for example, illustrate the potential of instructional technologies that enable workshops to overcome barriers of time, place, and pace, thus potentially reaching larger numbers of adult learners and more diverse populations than ever before. Responsible practice, however, mandates that we not only increase accessibility of learning opportunities but also ensure that we are prepared to do so. These authors highlight the importance of the availability of support systems for learners and instructors that will ensure that the use of technology leads to successful learning, not simply increased access.

In contrast to learning at a distance is the intimate experience of learning in residence. The residential workshop is not new, nor is an awareness of its unique nature. Bersch and I suggest, however, that the residential workshop may have particular significance in current times, because it has the potential to help offset the impersonality of our lives and the limited time we have available for formal learning. As we live and work ever more separately from one another, there is at the same time a growing need for being connected. Residential workshops have the potential to nurture these connections. We must continue to question, however, how well prepared we are to consistently provide the intensity of experience that has always been associated with learning and living together.

Another facet of workshops that is certainly not new but that may have new significance is learning in small groups. The use of small groups has become even more important to illustrate the potential of workshops to meet current demands for teamwork, communication, and creative, collaborative problem solving. Will notes that a particular challenge for the workshop facilitator is to remain flexible, even when faced with the pressures of limited time and demands for specific outcomes. The questions here focus on our ability to be sensitive to both the dynamics and potential of group process to allow groups to develop their own character and engage in the creation of shared knowledge.

Concluding Comments

In the preceding chapter, Hentschel provided a revealing look at the real-life beliefs and behaviors of an experienced workshop planner and facilitator. Her concluding comments have led me to suggest that there is, perhaps, a basic thematic element that must run throughout our planning, design, facilitation, and evaluation of workshops. That element is passion. And the authors of this sourcebook are passionate. It is this trait that has allowed them to see an old workhorse with new eyes and to find value in critically examining how well we understand the ways in which it is affected by social, political, and ethical concerns. These authors have looked at the workshop for what it is: a complex undertaking with layers of contextual influences and with vast potential to meet diverse adult needs and societal demands. If not taken for granted, the critically examined workshop will remain the dependable workhorse of adult and continuing education practice for years to come.

JEAN ANDERSON FLEMING is assistant professor of adult and community education at Ball State University, Muncie, Indiana.

INDEX

ORDERING INFORMATION

NEW DIRECTIONS FOR ADULT AND CONTINUING EDUCATION is a series of paperback books that explores issues of common interest to instructors, administrators, counselors, and policy makers in a broad range of adult and continuing education settings—such as colleges and universities, extension programs, businesses, the military, prisons, libraries, and museums. Books in the series are published quarterly in Spring, Summer, Fall, and Winter and are available for purchase by subscription and individually.

SUBSCRIPTIONS cost $54.00 for individuals (a savings of 35 percent over single-copy prices) and $90.00 for institutions, agencies, and libraries. Standing orders are accepted. New York residents, add local sales tax for subscriptions. (For subscriptions outside the United States, add $7.00 for shipping via surface mail or $25.00 for air mail. Orders must be prepaid in U.S. dollars by check drawn on a U.S. bank or charged to VISA, MasterCard, or American Express.)

SINGLE COPIES cost $22.00 plus shipping (see below) when payment accompanies order. California, New Jersey, New York, and Washington, D.C., residents, please include appropriate sales tax. Canadian residents, add GST and any local taxes. Billed orders will be charged shipping and handling. No billed shipments to post office boxes. (Orders from outside the United States must be prepaid in U.S. dollars by check drawn on a U.S. bank or charged to VISA, MasterCard, or American Express.)

SHIPPING (SINGLE COPIES ONLY): $30.00 and under, add $5.50; to $50.00, add $6.50; to $75.00, add $7.50; to $100.00, add $9.00; to $150.00, add $10.00.

ALL PRICES are subject to change.

DISCOUNTS FOR QUANTITY ORDERS are available. Please write to the address below for information.

ALL ORDERS must include either the name of an individual or an official purchase order number. Please submit your order as follows:
   Subscriptions: specify series and year subscription is to begin
   Single copies: include individual title code (such as ACE 59)

MAIL ALL ORDERS TO:
Jossey-Bass Publishers
350 Sansome Street
San Francisco, CA 94104-1342

Phone subscriptions or single-copy orders toll-free at (888) 378-2537 or at (415) 433-1767 (toll call).
Fax orders toll-free to: (800) 605-2665.

FOR SUBSCRIPTION SALES OUTSIDE OF THE UNITED STATES, contact any international subscription agency or Jossey-Bass directly.

OTHER TITLES AVAILABLE IN THE NEW DIRECTIONS FOR
ADULT AND CONTINUING EUCATION SERIES
Ralph G. Brockett, Susan Imel, Editors-in-Chief

Statement of Ownership, Management, and Circulation

(Required by 39 USC 3685)

1. Publication Title	2. Publication Number									3. Filing Date
NEW DIRECTIONS FOR ADULT AND CONTINUING EDUCATION	0	1	9	5	.	2	2	4	2	9/26/97

4. Issue Frequency	5. Number of Issues Published Annually	6. Annual Subscription Price
QUARTERLY	4	$54 - indiv. $90 - instit.

7. Complete Mailing Address of Known Office of Publication *(Not printer) (Street, city, county, state, and ZIP+4)*	Contact Person
350 SANSOME STREET SAN FRANCISCO, CA 94104 (SAN FRANCISCO COUNTY)	ROGER HUNT Telephone 415 782 3232

8. Complete Mailing Address of Headquarters or General Business Office of Publisher *(Not printer)*

SAME AS ABOVE

9. Full Names and Complete Mailing Addresses of Publisher, Editor, and Managing Editor *(Do not leave blank)*

Publisher *(Name and complete mailing address)*

JOSSEY-BASS INC., PUBLISHERS
(ABOVE ADDRESS)

Editor *(Name and complete mailing address)* SUSAN IMEL, CTR FOR TRAINING & EMPLOYMENT
OHIO STATE UNIVERSITY
1900 KENNY ROAD
COLUMBUS, OH 43210-1090

Managing Editor *(Name and complete mailing address)*

NONE

10. Owner *(Do not leave blank. If the publication is owned by a corporation, give the name and address of the corporation immediately followed by the names and addresses of all stockholders owning or holding 1 percent or more of the total amount of stock. If not owned by a corporation, give the names and addresses of the individual owners. If owned by a partnership or other unincorporated firm, give its name and address as well as those of each individual owner. If the publication is published by a nonprofit organization, give its name and address.)*

Full Name	Complete Mailing Address
SIMON & SCHUSTER, INC.	P.O. BOX 1172
	ENGLEWOOD CLIFFS, NJ 07632-1172

11. Known Bondholders, Mortgagees, and Other Security Holders Owning or Holding 1 Percent or More of Total Amount of Bonds, Mortgages, or Other Securities. If none, check box — ▶ ☐ None

Full Name	Complete Mailing Address
SAME AS ABOVE	SAME AS ABOVE

12. Tax Status *(For completion by nonprofit organizations authorized to mail at special rates) (Check one)*
The purpose, function, and nonprofit status of this organization and the exempt status for federal income tax purposes:
☐ Has Not Changed During Preceding 12 Months
☐ Has Changed During Preceding 12 Months *(Publisher must submit explanation of change with this statement)*

PS Form **3526**, September 1995 *(See Instructions on Reverse)*

13. Publication Title	14. Issue Date for Circulation Data Below
NEW DIRECTIONS FOR ADULT AND CONTINUING EDUCATION	SPRING 1997

15.

Extent and Nature of Circulation		Average No. Copies Each Issue During Preceding 12 Months	Actual No. Copies of Single Issue Published Nearest to Filing Date
a. Total Number of Copies *(Net press run)*		1610	1628
b. Paid and/or Requested Circulation	(1) Sales Through Dealers and Carriers, Street Vendors, and Counter Sales *(Not mailed)*	199	65
	(2) Paid or Requested Mail Subscriptions *(Include advertiser's proof copies and exchange copies)*	718	714
c. Total Paid and/or Requested Circulation *(Sum of 15b(1) and 15b(2))* ▶		917	779
d. Free Distribution by Mail *(Samples, complimentary, and other free)*		0	0
e. Free Distribution Outside the Mail *(Carriers or other means)*		185	124
f. Total Free Distribution *(Sum of 15d and 15e)* ▶		185	124
g. Total Distribution *(Sum of 15c and 15f)* ▶		1102	903
h. Copies not Distributed	(1) Office Use, Leftovers, Spoiled	508	725
	(2) Returns from News Agents	0	0
i. Total *(Sum of 15g, 15h(1), and 15h(2))* ▶		1610	1628
Percent Paid and/or Requested Circulation *(15c / 15g x 100)*		83%	86%

16. Publication of Statement of Ownership
☒ Publication required. Will be printed in the WINTER 1997 issue of this publication.
☐ Publication not required.

17. Signature and Title of Editor, Publisher, Business Manager, or Owner

SUSAN E. LEWIS
PERIODICALS DIRECTOR

Date 9/25/97

I certify that all information furnished on this form is true and complete. I understand that anyone who furnishes false or misleading information on this form or who omits material or information requested on the form may be subject to criminal sanctions (including fines and imprisonment) and/or civil sanctions (including multiple damages and civil penalties).

Instructions to Publishers

1. Complete and file one copy of this form with your postmaster annually on or before October 1. Keep a copy of the completed form for your records.

2. In cases where the stockholder or security holder is a trustee, include in items 10 and 11 the name of the person or corporation for whom the trustee is acting. Also include the names and addresses of individuals who are stockholders who own or hold 1 percent or more of the total amount of bonds, mortgages, or other securities of the publishing corporation. In item 11, if none, check the box. Use blank sheets if more space is required.

3. Be sure to furnish all circulation information called for in item 15. Free circulation must be shown in items 15d, e, and f.

4. If the publication had second-class authorization as a general or requester publication, this Statement of Ownership, Management, and Circulation must be published; it must be printed in any issue in October or, if the publication is not published during October, the first issue printed after October.

5. In item 16, indicate the date of the issue in which this Statement of Ownership will be published.

6. Item 17 must be signed.

Failure to file or publish a statement of ownership may lead to suspension of second-class authorization.

PS Form **3526**, September 1995 *(Reverse)*